BOTH SIDES

WHEN THE DOCTOR BECOMES THE CANCER PATIENT

*A Doctor's Journey of Healing
Using Positive Thinking Cards
Through Breast Cancer
And Beyond*

Dr. Alexandra Ginty, M.D.
www.DrBothsides.com

authorHOUSE®

AuthorHouse™
1663 Liberty Drive
Bloomington, IN 47403
www.authorhouse.com
Phone: 1-800-839-8640

© 2013 Dr. Alexandra Ginty, M.D. CCFP(EM) FCFP. All rights reserved.

No part of this book may be reproduced, stored in a retrieval system, or transmitted by any means without the written permission of the author.

Published by AuthorHouse 12/18/2013

ISBN: 978-1-4918-1227-3 (sc)
ISBN: 978-1-4918-1226-6 (hc)
ISBN: 978-1-4918-1225-9 (e)

Library of Congress Control Number: 2013915106

Any people depicted in stock imagery provided by Thinkstock are models, and such images are being used for illustrative purposes only. Certain stock imagery © Thinkstock.

This book is printed on acid-free paper.

Because of the dynamic nature of the Internet, any web addresses or links contained in this book may have changed since publication and may no longer be valid. The views expressed in this work are solely those of the author and do not necessarily reflect the views of the publisher, and the publisher hereby disclaims any responsibility for them.

This book is dedicated to

Mark

Not all heroes wear capes

Contents

Both Sides xi
Introduction xiii
Inspiration xv
The Story xvii
The Biology of Happiness xxxi

SECTION 1 – SELF REFLECTION

Positive Thinking Card 1 1
I Am 3
Be Your Authentic Self 5
New Me 6
If your Tears Had A Voice, What Would They Say? 7
My Journey 8
Courage 10
Peace 11
Be A Yes Man 12
My Path 13
The Mask 15
Footprints In The Sand 17
What Has Cancer Taught Me? 18
The Light And The Shadow 19
Trust Is The Opposite Of Fear 21
Believe 22
The Outsider 23

SECTION 2 – SUPPORT

Positive Thinking Card 2 27
Support 28
The Pyramid of Support 30
Look In Your Village 32

SECTION 3 – BACK TO WORK

Positive Thinking Card 3 37
My Team 39
Making A Difference 40
A Hospital Journey 41

SECTION 4 – MOTIVATION

Positive Thinking Card 4 45
No Excuses 48
Motivation Poem 50
ABCs Of Moving On 51
Energy 53
It's Not Just About Winning 55
Lessons From Snowboarding 57
No Should-ing Allowed 59
The Power Of Great Feelings 61
Don't Be Afraid to Try; Just Modify 63
Positive Thinking 64
Inner Strength – Find Your Greatness 65
What I Would Put In My Awesome Day? 67
What I Learned From Others 68
GrrrAttitude 70
Vitamin G Today 71

SECTION 5 – BALANCE

Positive Thinking Card 5 77
Balance 78
Grace 80
Fatigue 81
Quiet Time 83
Grounding 85
Time 86
When Are You Better? 87
Today 88

The Lake 89
Gardening 91
Let's Talk About Stress 92

SECTION 6 – FAMILY

Positive Thinking Card 6 97
Every Fighter Pilot Needs A Good Wingman 100
How Do You Tell Kids About Cancer? 101
Family Poem 103
How Cancer Changes Us – A Teen's Perspective: 104
Nano – My Dog 107

SECTION 7 – FRIENDS

Positive Thinking Card 7 111
Friends 113
Dear Friend 114
3 Friends 116

SECTION 8 – DIFFICULT THINGS

Positive Thinking Card 8 119
Control – Learning Not To Have It All 120
Think Before You Talk, But Please Talk 122
Say The Word "Mastectomies" 126
Love Our Flaws – They Make Us Unique. 127
Hair – Day 16 128
Everyone Has A Story 129
When You Can't Change The Outcome, You Can
    Change The Journey 131
Its Not What's Important, It's Who's Important 132
Dream 134
Cherish Each Moment 136

SECTION 9 – LOVE

Positive Thinking Card 9.. 139
Love Poem.. 140
Forever 141
I love 142

SECTION 10 – SURVIVORSHIP

Positive Thinking Card 10.. 147
What Is Survivorship?.. 148
The Most Beautiful Stones... 149
My Bucket List... 150
Are you a Survivor or even a Thriver?... 152
Relay for life 154
Growing Old Is A Beautiful Thing 155
Sparkle 156
Spirit 158
Only In The Darkness Are You Able To See The Stars.................. 159
You Can't Change The World – Not Everyone Is
    Ready To Listen... 161
Everything And Nothing... 163
Giving back 166
The "Used to" Person.. 168
Define Yourself.. 169
Cut And Keep 172

Notes and Quotes 183
Acknowledgements... 189
Appendix of Medical Terms... 191

Both Sides

From the start it was clear that if I could get through
This journey would teach me more than I knew
I'd be the voice of a patient in pain
As I've heard the word cancer, I couldn't retain
I felt the sweat of terrible fear
And seen a world that all goes unclear
Felt the drains that hung by my side
My colleagues as experts to use as my guide
Going to areas not covered in books
Chemo and wig shops and changing your looks
Then the part that no on could see
With chemo came loss of memory
On the surface I functioned but anxious within
That my mind was too injured for work to begin
Discovering strength one step at a time
A journey that only the patient must climb,
Enduring this path was not just the goal
As a doctor my outlook had now touched my soul
To help all my patients as they struggle to see
How scary and overwhelming cancer can be
This is why Both Sides is where I now live
With scars as a patient and as a doctor now give

Introduction

It felt as though I was swimming for my life in a storm of bad news, barely able to keep my head above water before the next wave of bad news hit. As the painful emotions hurt, I could leave the suffering on paper. I never intended to read the words again – the therapy was in the unloading. My diary could take the anger and pain. You can't put that emotion on the ones you love.

As a family doctor facing bilateral breast cancer, I had to find a way forward. The mental anguish with so many waves of bad news is terrifying. I used my psychotherapy tools on myself. I developed positive thinking cards to help me think differently. Most of these lines were created when I met obstacles and tried to look at them in a different light. By writing constructive phrases, and repeating them in hard times, the trust and belief that you have strength is there. The positive phrases overcome the suffering – not an instant happiness, simply a confidence to believe that around the corner it will get better and the phrases help you stay on that path.

As cancer treatment ends, the comfort and support of frequent visits stops and you are on your own. It feels like the war is not over, yet everyone sees a "survivor," expecting a new normal. You feel far from that. Vulnerable and frightened, the confusion rules your mind. At these difficult points, my thinking cards helped reassure the thoughts of doubt and exhaustion to ones of belief and determination. It was about finding the motivation when you are scared and the perseverance in the weakest times. I learned to live in the present and reminded myself to notice my thoughts and find balance in the chaos.

It was at these points of irritability and anxiety that I found art therapy. There was an apprehension to disclose my feelings in case of repercussions, both personally and professionally, yet this was too big to deal with alone. These were new boundaries for me.

There is a catharsis as the emotional mind connects with the hand – a freedom to release bad feelings of uncertainty. As I looked at the pictures afterwards, the powerful artwork explained my pain, often accompanied with tears of loss. This process is part of the healing.

The poems are emotional messages to the world and mantras of encouragement to myself. It shows that there is a warrior in all of us. That strength can be great and see us through the toughest times – the ones that no one could ever imagine – the ones that blindside you again and again until you feel you can't get up.

This is a handbook of positive thinking to help you think differently. I hope it will be bookmarked, stuffed into the chemo bag or on a dresser, knowing that when it is a tough day, you will remember to turn to that poem or chapter that helps you stay grounded and allows you to turn your thinking around. It is a handbook worth sharing for all of life's adversities.

Inspiration

Inspiration is a spirit
That dwells in the heart of perseverance
A smile that shines through adversity
A foot that steps into fear
A scarf that says I'm me
And no one can take that away
Scars of silent courage
Reports of cancer, not to define you
Strength to go on when weakened
Resilience to find happiness
Attitude to wear pink
Gratitude that friends are always there
Belief that we have purpose
Not to be too proud to admit weaknesses
No need to compare to understand
Passion to share the joy of life
Fulfillment to get back what was taken away
Arms to wrap around your family
Endurance to last the course
An outlook to celebrate milestones, however small
Confidence that pales physical changes
Compassion that stings because you have been there
Not afraid to face what you are missing
Because you realize what you bring
An ear to listen and share the burden
Enthusiasm that is infectious
Respect that connects colleagues
Willpower to go beyond your comfort zone
Motivation that creates followers
A voice to tell the world what they don't see.

The Story

I now know that I am here with purpose. To look terrified patients in the eye and hold their hand through surgery and treatments, knowing I have felt that pain and fear, crosses barriers. The ability to be there for them is inspiration and hope beyond their disease. The phrases I use from my positive thinking cards ring in my head to find strength and refocus in difficult times. Life just looks different now. Hopefully, you will find this too.

You may feel too fragile to read the excerpts of my story though we all walk in different shoes with different burdens; it may sting because you have been there and you feel the kinship; or this may help you to feel what it is like to experience a shattering diagnosis. It is a mental journey of survival that takes every cell of determination to climb out of the darkness when you have been knocked so far down.

For some, you may want to skip the pain of hearing or comparing to any other cancer. I remember and respect that feeling of survival. For others, it is hard to see the journey of healing without the story.

* * *

Diary
April 2010

There it was. Why hadn't I noticed it? An egg shaped mass in my left breast. I was not too concerned but decided to head to the hospital in the morning.

* * *

One of the clues of impending disaster came when the radiologist asked me if I had spoken to a surgeon. I told him that I was just about to call the surgeon who saved me from my ruptured appendix 5 years earlier. The radiologist then said that he would page the surgeon for me and I could call his office for an appointment. I was naively grateful.

In bed that night, I couldn't sleep. My brain kept practicing what it would be like to hear the word cancer in case it was. That way, I thought,

I would have heard it before and it wouldn't sound so bad. I kept trying to say it to myself but something in me just wouldn't listen. Deep down, I didn't want to acknowledge it but knew that it was not an ordinary case after five hours of workup in radiology that day.

* * *

My surgeon paged me – there it was, his number. I was in the middle of a ten-hour office day. "It is cancer," he said. It was like nothing else existed. I was listening to a doctor talk about a patient, something I did all the time. It couldn't be me. I want it out but he insisted an MRI was recommended with my findings to check some other areas. He offered to tell my husband. I was so grateful.

My father was already in chemo and had a lung removal for cancer, two months earlier. How was my mother going to manage?

The report is on my desk at home. I sign off those reports every day, but to see my name on it was surreal.

* * *

So the biopsy gun went in again as the MRI found another tumour in the right breast. I wanted information but all I got were the routine words of uncertainty. For the second time that week, they froze and cut the skin and I watched as the gun hit the tumour against my chest wall. It felt like a bullet jarred my chest wall. A part of me felt that the likelihood of having two cancers at once was so low that I took it in stride; shivering and trying to sort out the emotional chaos I was going through.

* * *

My head went down – BOTH SIDES!!!! I could feel that hot rush up my cheeks and icy stunned disbelief. "It is multifocal, not metastases," the surgeon said. "Bad breast tissue." "What do we do now," I asked desperately. I had to get rid of all this. "Yes, you can say it," he said seriously. "Mastectomies?" Time slowed down as I looked at the yellow walls. He waited for my answer. I was alone, searching for that person in me who makes critical decisions, as an emergency room physician. After the silent pause, I told him that I had always said that if you cut off my arm, I would still be Alex and I will do what I have to do to get rid of these cancers.

I feel like any minute I am going to wake up from this horrible nightmare. I can't get my feet under me. I feel like I'm in an avalanche and every time I think I can take a breath, I'm knocked down again. I'm losing trust that it will be all right. I am desperate to find control.

I came out of the building, my head spinning like a tornado, bright sunlight made me feel alive but inside I was numb. I found my friend and held her hand like I would drown if I didn't hold on. I called my husband.

* * *

The days that followed were a blur. I met with the plastic surgeon about planning reconstruction. She was planning to put implants under the chest muscle using graft material to ensure coverage. On the left side, the cancer was bigger and may only leave enough skin for a tissue expander. We would be prepared for everything. The day of surgery was an early appointment for bilateral radioactive dye injections into both breasts near each cancer tumour. The surgeon had decided that the double dose was allowed and the dye used in the operation to locate the draining nodes in each armpit would be as limited as possible in dose. Then up to the admissions area and back over to the plastic surgeon for surgical markings. Finally, back to the surgical waiting room and I gladly took the pre-surgical medication that I was offered. The next few days were going to be very tough.

* * *

It was pain that recalibrated anything imaginable. I awoke the day after the five hour surgery in so much pain that my hand could not get to the pump to release some pain medication. I felt like I had been run over by a truck on my chest. I swayed in narcotic nausea as I looked at my wrapped chest in the mirror. They had put in full implants.

A remarkable thing happened that day. It is about saying "Yes" when you want to curl up and hide. As I was so sick in the hospital bed, a friend asked me if I wanted the help of a special person who had helped him. I had decided to say "Yes" to everything – meals, help, everything. A very special minister called to help me through my journey. I thought I didn't really need this, not my style so I explained in every way that this was not necessary. "I could manage, it was not that bad." He would not take no for an answer and I was about to discover a person who helped me think differently, spiritually and philosophically, exploring the present and noticing it, allowing me to grieve, normalize my doubts and find my strengths to believe that I can be open to change. He just listened and reflected.

* * *

May 2010

"I'm going to be brutally honest though, it makes the picture a little more negative and means chemotherapy," the surgeon said. I already had my head around that but hated it when he used words like "survival rate."

We know that it is invasive cancer on both sides now – Invasive Ductal Carcinoma on left, Invasive Tubular Carcinoma on right with many areas of Ductal Carcinoma In-Situ bilaterally, involving a node on the left. What a death sentence.

I am suddenly jolted back into the mental world of dealing with cancer and the unknown again. It is so hard to focus on the future and remain optimistic. People say I am brave but on the inside I feel so afraid of what they are going to say next. Just as I get my hopes positive in my head, I am knocked down again. It is very, very hard and mentally exhausting on this roller coaster.

* * *

I have had a hard time adjusting to my thoughts. I thought to myself, "I've had enough now, I want to get off this train," but it does not stop. The only path is straight through. My first tears.

* * *

I am angry at the moment. I am angry for recognizing that it is not behind me yet, that I am a statistical stage of medical survival when in my heart, that is not a place that I will let myself think about. I start to get extremely anxious thinking about staging the cancer and talking about it. Up until now, it was like I had my appendectomy and next week I would be better. A little medicine and I will be on with the rest of my life. It is not like that. This alien-like disease is sinister, quiet and deadly. There are so many unknowns that you don't always trust your own feelings anymore since I have been hurt so many times in the last few weeks.

* * *

I saw two oncologists this week who told us the most important news – that review of the pathology has determined the left node to be positive. The pathology review also staged the left cancer as the most aggressive level, which is not so good. This does not change the indication for radiation but means that he cannot proceed until a surgical full axillary dissection is done. More surgery!! – I am sure it will not be anything like the pain of this bilateral mastectomy with full reconstruction and bilateral sentinel node dissections that still burns so badly that it is consuming my thoughts.

I called my surgeon: he said that's the way it is and more surgery would be booked in the next few weeks.

* * *

June 2010

No further positive nodes so on we go with treatment. My oncologist discussed the 18 weeks of chemotherapy, gave me a binder of helpful information and all the programs that they offer and a requisition for a bone scan. It was quite overwhelming. I don't think I remember anything. Mark and I went to the wig shop and I booked an appointment to return with my friend since I need a little humour to deal with these things though something in me, my determination, makes me face every step face on without feeling sorry for myself.

* * *

I am now 6 weeks post-op double mastectomy for two cancers with reconstruction and bilateral sentinel node removal. It is now 2 weeks post-op total removal of all 9 remaining armpit lymph nodes (complete axillary dissection). A large seroma (fluid collection), the size of a large tangerine in my left armpit, drained 100cc in two massive syringes last Wednesday and it is still sore and I am unable to get my arm by my side. I went back today for another draining – 60 cc this time and still no lymphedema at the moment – that's good. He cautioned me about the risk of infection with upcoming chemo but I was confident it would be OK.

* * *

June 2 -Day 1 Chemo

It was an exhausting morning. I was given intravenous steroids but, despite that, this first regimen was very nauseating. The pharmacist discussed the drug side effects to expect over the next few days. The nurse was gowned with a mask similar to the operating room and thick gloves to protect her from the chemotherapy agents. I was instructed to suck ice chips to decrease mouth sores, so I had to pass on the nice soup offerings from the volunteer. The Epirubicin is called the "red devil" because it looks so evil. Huge syringes of the cold red poison were slowly injected over 30 minutes. This was primarily responsible for the hair loss and severe side effects. There were 2 other chemotherapy drugs, 5-Fluorouracil and Cyclophosphamide following that and then on to the pharmacy to collect all the medications for nausea and pain.

* * *

4 Days Post Chemo Round 1

I am now so exhausted. I slept and slept the last few days. My mouth is bone dry and I woke with excruciating chest pain as the Neulasta (white blood cell stimulator) reactivates all my recent surgery, which was so huge. I pulled myself to a hot shower but could barely eat with the nausea from pain medication.

If this is the beginning, I am rather afraid of what I face but I keep focusing on today only and do not let myself jump to the future. My mind is foggy – it is hard to think or calculate, with a constant headache.

I need the house quiet all the time, which is hard on the kids. I try to walk every day, no matter what. The kids still want normality and are impatient waiting for their needs.

I am too tired and do not have the energy for people to visit. Even answering the phone or writing this is a great effort. I never like wasting moments so it is hard for me to give in. I am scared for the next four months of this and even the next few weeks with all the changes it brings. My hair loss is going to be difficult for me to look at. It is still hard to believe this is happening – like being swept up in a big wave and my feet have still not touched the bottom.

My mother called today – I envied the energy in her voice and enthusiasm for jobs that I always have too. I want that person back as soon as possible – one foot in front of the other. One day at a time.

* * *

Day 16 Post Chemo 1

My hair fell out today. I went for a swim and wiped my head with my towel and it was covered in hair. With my squeaky wet hands, I wiped my head and looked at the huge amount of hair in my hand. I kept doing that and more and more hair came off in my hand. I went in the shower then looked in the mirror – it was all patchy; less hair on the sides. It was quite surreal. I didn't like the look but was also fascinated at the appearance since I was expecting it. Putting on a scarf, it felt like this was the beginning of the expected changes. There was a part of me that knew people could now physically see how hard this was – not just inside my head and under my clothes. I was more comfortable with these changes than my kids. My son was devastatingly embarrassed and did not want to see it and instructed me to always wear a wig. He does like my wig. It is very pretty. It only takes a minute to do my hair now and I had always wanted straight hair – now I can pretend. My husband is very accepting and says that if you smile you always look better. So that is my approach – I am going to smile, even when it is hard, in order to get through this. My scalp feels sticky smooth – quite weird.

* * *

August 2010
4 days Post Chemo Round 5

I am now day 4 after changing to a new chemo drug, Taxotere. During these treatments, my hands are wrapped in ice packs to decrease side effects to the fingers. The cold temperature aches my hands and I wrap myself with blankets and scarves. The steroid treatment has now stopped which feels like 10 cups of coffee. Now, the tiredness is really hitting me. I feel lightheaded, shaky and flushed. I have lost all taste except salt, which we laugh about. I am very achy.

The pain is so distracting that it makes me quite sick. It is very penetrating and I cannot touch my back, lying horizontal due to the dizziness and nausea. The world spins when I get up. This drug sucks every drop of energy from you. I can eat very little except rice and water. Lemon tastes really good. Coffee only has a bitter taste so that is off the menu. Peanut butter only tastes of oil and applesauce is tasteless. Clear salty soups are my favourite.

* * *

14 Days Post Chemo Round 5

To let you know that my energy is now back. This is my good week. I am out of the cocoon of nausea and pain. I am able to play tennis though a little more short of breath. I make up for that with hitting the ball with all my emotions.

* * *

Genetics
September 1 2010

I went to genetics today with a friend for memory and support since I felt exhausted from my recent chemo but I needed to go to this appointment. I was not feeling well at all this morning with headache and nausea before

I went out. My mouth hurts with a ridge of sores, making it so painful to eat anything. I have lost all taste except bitter, so that is all I can taste at the moment, like bile at the back of my throat. Cheese, yoghurt and bananas go down well. Yesterday I had a sip of wine and my whole mouth felt like it was on fire and my oesophagus was burning. My oncologist gave me a mouth rinse, which works well but wears off quickly, tasting of a very bad artificial flavour. My gums feel rough and swollen.

I had been flagged for genetics due to the fact that I had 2 primary simultaneous breast cancers – very rare. That alone, is enough to warrant genetic testing. I questioned my family history further from my father and discovered that my grandmother had died of inoperable ovarian cancer rather than the nonspecific "womb" cancer previously told. My father then pointed out that his mother knew she would die since both of her sisters had died a few years earlier of the same ovarian cancer presenting in the same manner. Adding to the picture of this small family, I was reminded that my cousin got ovarian cancer last year too. The picture was ominously coming together.

It wasn't too surprising therefore that the genetic counsellor explained how it is near impossible for my situation not to be genetic. The likelihood of two invasive different cancers appearing together is so low and the mechanism would lead us to assume that I have a genetic mutation in the repair protein such as BRCA1 or BRCA2 (BReast CAncer repair protein genes 1 and 2). Only up to 10 % of breast cancers are genetic and only a small percentage of these are BRCA mutations.

It was quite clear from this data, that she would advise me to have my ovaries out. Who would have thought that in that split second decision that I made, that it was so important to have done the mastectomies? My chance of ovarian cancer would drop 90% with hysterectomy and oophorectomy, leaving a small chance of ovarian cancer on the peritoneum only. It is a difficult cancer to detect early so the ovary removal was recommended.

* * *

I met with a gynaecologist and all the genetic data. He agreed. My oncologist, however, went a step further and recommended a hysterectomy rather than an oophorectomy since the drugs to treat me afterwards have a risk of endometrial cancer, which would be reduced with the full surgery.

I could tell the stress was getting to my husband. He couldn't bear another surgery and the worry. He was so frustrated that it is still not over. I reassured him that it would be finished soon. We must be patient. I asked my oncologist when was the soonest that I could have surgery after chemotherapy. He told me that I have to wait 6 weeks after the last dose to let my immunity recover so I booked my hysterectomy for 6 weeks to the day after my last Taxotere dose.

* * *

The genetic testing examined all of my genes for mutations, specifically BRCA ones. This detailed testing takes 4-6 months. It was clear that I would make my surgical decision based on the genetic counselling advice but I gave my blood for the BRCA testing too. This would help me know risks to my family and possibly other cancer risks for myself. I sent all this information to my cousin who had the same grandmother and had ovarian cancer herself. Uninterested before my diagnosis in her risk, they now looked at her case differently and she too got BRCA testing to evaluate her breast cancer risk if positive. What a lot of impact this is having. It is feeling like I am passing a deadly virus around to all these lovely people whose lives I have now put into a tailspin. My cousin was distressed to have dealt with her cancer, only to realize she was facing more decisions. I am proud of how everyone is facing reality to decrease his or her risks. It is easy to pretend that it will not happen to you, but it does.

* * *

October 2010

This was a total abdominal hysterectomy with bilateral oophorectomy and removal of unclassified right armpit nodule. I arrived in diagnostic imaging to do the usual wire insertion. It was another two-surgeon surgery.

It was a tough hospital stay this time. The worst was the severe nausea and dizziness. It was like riding an upside down roller coaster and the spinning never ending. I remember saying, "please make this stop."

* * *

January 05 2011

That was what I was, a genetic time bomb! It was New Year's Eve. I got a message that my genetics results were back and I had been fitted in for an appointment on Wednesday at noon. In fact, they phoned two more times to ensure that I was going to attend this meeting. As a physician, it is more than clear to me that when someone calls three times to ensure that I am fitted in to a noon appointment, it is a significant result. I had waited four months for this result and then three reminders for an appointment with two days notice over the holidays!

Yes, I was BRCA 1 positive – class 1 pathogenic/causal. It is a heterozygous mutation, so severe, that protein for repair of cell growth could not be made. Much like there was just no ending to the instruction book. It was described that I also tested positive for two BRCA 2 mutations but these were not significant and felt not contributory to the collection of mutated defense that my cells had.

I had done all the appropriate surgery; there was mutual respect by the surgeons, geneticists and oncologists to our decisions, which all proved right. What a journey unfolded. How did I make those high pressure decisions with little notice but somehow had enough knowledge and just knew deep inside me that it was the right decision. I recall feeling confident but overwhelmed like running a trauma – making big decisions in the heat of the moment because you have to decide and stick with it. I just knew that it was the right thing to do. I still shake my head at where I got that stamina. I still feel that a lot of good training kept me going in the difficult decision-making since it all happened so fast.

After explaining the results, I was asked if I needed a counsellor to discuss this unfortunate news. It affects my family significantly – 50:50 chance that my siblings or daughters or sons have this too. If you thought my journey has finished, it has just taken a break till the next wave of difficult stuff. All this is preventative however, including my abnormal colonoscopy that rose eyebrows! That is a big difference. My cousin who has gone through ovarian cancer last year is now planning her bilateral prophylactic mastectomy since she has tested positive for the same pathogenic BRCA 1 mutation. I can hardly believe this is all happening to me.

* * *

February 2011
Don't Let My Broken Arm Stop Me

As I went for that last run down the black diamond moguls in February I felt fearless. My cancer treatment just behind me, this was the trip I was waiting for, that carrot at the end of the long cancer road and nothing could compare to the feeling of ripping through that powder. It was 3 o'clock on the second day when I was in denial of my fatigue and missed the turn and tumbled, leaving my arm underneath me as a searing pain caught my arm. Not wanting to alarm anyone, my life had interrupted too many people already, so I put my arm against me, hanging there like a cut rope and carried on. The nausea was hitting me and unable to move my arm at all. My arm dangled by my side with no power but I couldn't resist the blue sky and took some more medications to venture back onto the hills with my arm in my pocket. The fractured humeral head was discovered a few days later and it was promptly immobilized for 6 weeks. Now I have my arm back moving again and strong with intense physiotherapy – the same arm as my axillary dissection had seized closed again. Who believes I can get back on that tennis court again? I have to. Wow this is hard. Pain is so tiring.

March 2012

It is the 3rd month of 2012, five months since my last anaesthetic for an urgent gall bladder surgery and hernia surgery and exactly 1 year since my broken left shoulder and 15 months since the end of cancer treatment and various treatments and splints for inflammatory arthritis. It is also only 4 months since the passing of my mother-in-law as cancer quickly took her life despite all efforts. I was tired but this one was looking like a good clear year.

It was a gorgeous day on the lake, completely frozen all over as far as the eye could see. The kids were away and one of those weekend escapes at our cottage. We went for a walk but the ice was too inviting for my husband – we would go back and put on skates.

I know my bones are fragile from anti-estrogen medications to keep the cancers away. My husband assured me that holding a hockey stick would add stability. The ice was very hard and bumpy. About ½ km out on the lake, after a split second of loosing my balance, I instinctively put out my left hand. As I fell, I watched it bend further than any hand should. A shooting pain went up my arm and I knew.

There was only one way back to the cottage – skating back with my broken arm. Any wobble and the pain screamed as I could feel how loose my wrist was. I took off my coat and saw the S-shape in my forearm.

It was angulated and very broken in lots of pieces and needed reducing (straightening) under anaesthetic. So I resigned myself to this year's procedure and was put asleep as they pulled it straight and moulded a cast to keep it there.

It is now in an awkward cast that tilts the wrist to make it very difficult to use. My fingers look like sausages and my rings now live on my necklace for a while.

Again, I'm off the tennis courts, so on with the art classes. The nausea and pain made work very challenging in the beginning. My make up is not as good and my hair has taken on a natural look, but back I will come back. There is more painful physiotherapy ahead in the same arm as the broken shoulder and axillary dissection scarring. Getting back to tennis is really hard this time – a very mental journey of determination.

Dig deep for determination. Believe in yourself when others don't. Who said it was easy?

And so more positive thinking cards were made.

The Biology of Happiness

It is said that once you have enough money for essential things in life, that happiness does not get greater with external possessions. Happiness comes from within. 50% of our happiness is predetermined, genetic; 10% is situational – life circumstances, your job and 40% is changeable or modifiable – your attitude and how you decide to look at things. Happier people feel more fulfilled.

Being happy and laughing, we produce good hormones – dopamine, serotonin, oxytocin and norepinephrine. These cell hormones help to address the stress response. Learning to think differently can change the amounts of these hormones. Higher levels of these hormones can reduce pain. Aerobic exercise is excellent at producing these hormones too. They have a direct impact in the brain to improve mood and optimism.

It is because of this biology that we do better after adversity. Mixing with good friends and taking steps towards some physical activity will pump out the good endorphins and change your mood. It is noted also that those people with good supports have better outcomes through adversity, and take next steps with more confidence.

Endorphins play a role in pain control. Pain has many components including emotional pain. If we don't address all parts of pain control, then we will not completely deal with it. Controlling physical pain is only one part of pain management – sometimes a concept overlooked.

It is also noticed that there is a state that people can reach where your thoughts are uninterrupted and the mind is happily concentrating. I call it "The place in your head where time stands still" – doing art or tennis or, for some, it is music or running. It has been called "Flow," producing good endorphins like meditation.

How can we do this? Activate your internal locus of control – The "I can do it" or determination part of you and learn to love and believe in the new and wonderful person that you are.

Hang out with positive people,
Meet a friend for coffee and laugh till your cheeks hurt

Connect via email, facebook, twitter so that you are not alone
Journal and post quotes to live by
Find the good in a situation, no matter how hard – re-framing
Focus life to living in the present
Take the tough climb, one step at a time
Try new things or hobbies; go outside comfort zones
Walk new routes
Walk, elliptical, stationary bike
Flow
Mindfulness and meditation in movement, hobbies, yoga and other challenging exercises
Help others & give back, fundraise, volunteer
Support, support, support
Strengths come from exposing weaknesses
Believe that we have purpose
Count your blessings
Forgiveness
Admire the good in others
DECIDE TO BE HAPPY – IT'S CONTAGIOUS

SECTION 1

Self Reflection

Positive Thinking Card 1

> **Things to Remember**
>
> Laugh at myself. Laugh at mistakes. Get up, put make up on, show-up for life. Exercise. Enjoy every moment, live for today. Laugh again. Don't sweat the small stuff. **If it didn't hurt anyone, leave it in the past.** Worry only about the things that you can change. Don't complain – take a pill. Ask for help. Order it online when you feel lousy. Play tennis. **Talk to those people who make you feel good.** Laugh at those cravings. Remember your eyebrow pencil in your purse. There's always a way. Play the cards you are dealt. Perseverance. Love your job, if you don't, change it. Control stress. **When it upsets you, write it down, it works.** Heal thyself mentally too, chemo fog is real. Make lists. Make to do lists. **Smile, you look better.** Put away the black clothes. Say yes more than you want to, you'll be surprised at the results. Swim. Remember the best people in the world and how much they are there for you, always and always.

The purpose of this book is to help people out of adversity, particularly the terrible fragility and fear that accompanies cancer with its many blows of bad news that can knock your confidence and trust so far down. This is about how to notice those intrusive thoughts of doubt and fear and battle them against positive ones.

My positive thinking cards started with my embarrassingly forgetful chemo-brain. I could not multi-task. Not everyone could see it, but inside my head it felt as if all the information files had been scattered all over the floor. I could not find words – I could talk around a topic but inside I was panicking. I was used to a mind that worked so fast. Forgetting things actually became very scary, thinking that I could not possibly function as a physician with this memory. I set up a chalkboard and wrote everything down. I set up lists and made reminders in my phone. I had to be reassured that it was temporary, to "Laugh at my mistakes". So I started the thinking cards. It was a way of forgiving my inadequacy to replace them with thoughts of kindness and constructive change. I did not want to always talk about my consuming mastectomy and reconstruction pain or how nauseous, tired and sick I felt – pulling others down was the last thing I wanted. "Don't complain, take a pill" was created. As I battled the symptoms, instead of complaining, the words would recite themselves and I would go and take some medication, which helped everyone. On the way to physiotherapy, for terrible armpit scarring after the lymph node surgery, I stopped at a shop to try on clothes. This was a feat in itself, since my chest was so painful. As I looked in the mirror, I had erased one of my pencilled eyebrows. Only one remained. "Always carry your eyebrow pencil in your purse" was a humorous reminder of my efforts to look normal. Asking for help is one of the hardest things in treatment. It involves admitting weakness – that you can't do it. It is the loss of pride that is so hard.

Afraid of chemo and the physical changes and hair loss that accompany it, I worried if I would be loved the same way. "Just smile" was the message I was given – that brings out the inner spirit. It worked, no matter how hard the moment was, I held my head high and smiled and people noticed and smiled back or commented on how good I looked. That was all I needed. "Smile, you look better" was the positive thinking I kept when facing any difficult hurdle – not always smiling on the inside but a path to feeling better for that moment was welcomed. When terrifying things happen, there is an instinct to make safety fences and keep within them to protect you from further harm. It is difficult to do things outside your comfort zone. "Saying yes to more than I wanted to," gave me the confidence to step into the unknown, which usually resulted in good things happening.

As I went to my first chemo session, I thought I would be comfortable in my black yoga clothes. I looked around at the illness as we all sat with our infusions and refused to acknowledge the dark mood that went with it. I decided that I would only wear colour to reflect my mood – usually my favourite pink, always a cheerful colour to reflect how I intended to feel. So I "put away the black clothes."

These constructive thoughts were always in my head; I just had to learn to notice them. When I wrote down the first ones, the rest followed. Using these good phrases, I could learn to push myself, forgive the weaknesses, make goals for recovery and focus on balance.

I Am

This was my first poem, a discovery of my emotions. I attended a class called "Writing for The Health Of It" at Wellspring. I was very fragile and angry. I felt that no one could understand my trauma, mental anguish, loss of career and uncertainty. I was extremely nervous to be in a group where this comparison may be tested.

So, as the thinking card says, "Say yes more than you want to, you'll be surprised at the results." I went out of my comfort zone, knowing I could leave if I couldn't bear it.

I was to discover how I could release my feelings in words. An exercise called "I am" as the homework of week three changed everything. The first two words were established, the rest had to be my creation, the "I am" verse is repeating.

The response to the poem was remarkable. I realized how the expression of my pain could be heard and understood, yet always to find the positive side. This was the beginning of many more.

* * *

I Am
(Oct 2010)

I am persevering and strong
I wonder where my new path will take me
I hear the peace at my cottage – the water on the dock
I see the warm pink sunset flooding over us after a wonderful day
I want to keep it all safe so that nothing can take it away
I am persevering and strong

I pretend to have hair and look normal
I feel no one understands the scars and mental journey
I touch my husband's hand and want it to last forever
I worry that he has too much burden

I cry that my family love me so much and don't like me hurt
I am persevering and strong

I understand that we all have a destiny
I say that I must trust this path
I dream that I will make a difference to many
I try always to see the positive in everything
I hope never to forget how much can be taken away
I am persevering and strong

In comparison, I looked at this poem and rewrote it one year later, now back at work to see how I had changed – fascinating.

I Am
(Jan 2012)

I am passionate about life
I wonder what my future will be
I hear grounding words in my head whenever I am upset
I see the beauty in every moment, no matter how small
I want to fit everything in
I am passionate about life

I pretend that I don't think about cancer returning
I feel no one knows what goes on in my head
I touch people at a whole new level now
I worry how my kids will cope
I cry that this gene mutation is not the end of the story
I am passionate about life

I understand that there are statistics
I say to myself that looking after everyone includes me
I dream that I will do so much with what I have learned
I try to always see the positive in everything
I hope to be part of making this a treatable disease
I am passionate about life

Be Your Authentic Self

As I struggled with all the pieces of me that were taken away by cancer, there is resentment and anger to the loss of control, loss of identity, loss of perceived beauty and anger that no one else had gone through the same issues. In fact, I was angry that some of my friends or colleagues would juggle so many things and not be prepared for the fact that your whole world can come to a grinding halt.

A very good minister and counsellor gave me his time and patience to listen and reflect on my observations. He told me that all those things that I had lost were just clothes. If you look, you are still the same person who fought to get into medical school, learned to waterski by getting hypothermia with determination and someone fell in love with that, and friends respect you for that, not the clothes. The clothes will come back, he promised me that, but letting the real me shine through was so important, despite the changes.

Your authentic self is not the person you think you should be but the true and real you. It should be the same person at work, on the tennis court and at home – no hats. And so I examined my life, not to do what I should but to listen to my stamina and give and receive what was healthy for others and myself. This empowerment is satisfying. It is a decision to cut out negative and create positive, truthful thoughts to live by.

New Me

My heart is compassion, devotion and care
Learning to delegate, learning to share
If I'm not healthy then I can't be
A person to help in adversity

Remember when the going gets rough
That all you can do is always enough
Not to look back, just to move on
Only take wisdom from what has gone

True to myself will make me strong
And share my spirit all life long
Permission to change in order to be
A balanced person – that's the New Me

If your Tears Had A Voice, What Would They Say?

If your tears had a voice, what would they say
I'm scared and I'm human, hold me and stay
Be there when it hurts and decisions so tough
Those tears when I realize the pain is enough.

If your tears had a voice, what would they say
Don't hurt my family, for strength I now pray
Some think I'm strong – it's so big you can't see
Sometimes those tears are because I'm just me.

If your tears had a voice, what would they say
It took all my plans and innocence away
My art shows the fear and the tears gently flow
And I see through the healing that trust will now grow.

If your tears had a voice, what would they say
Do what you love and rejoice in each day
Crossing the finish line hands held high
Tears of happiness together we cry.

Now I can say there's a voice from the tears
Motivation for change from all those years
Determination, perseverance, tenacity's now me
Compassion, understanding on both sides I see
Immersed in such hardship it's hard to perceive
That life makes sense backwards if you believe.

My Journey

As a doctor, my breast lump was serious news
Tests and more tests were ominous clues
I knew in my mind the depth of concern
My gut told the story, afraid what I'd learn
It all was surreal as the phone call sank in
I had breast cancer – let the journey begin
MRI recall and testing right side
Both sides had cancer – and that's when I cried
I focused on progress, moving with pace
Like running a trauma emergency case
Together the surgeons worked to fix me
Reconstruction and double mastectomy
The result from the nodes hit like a ton
Removing more nodes had to be done
Wounds were still fresh and pain still so bad
But on went the surgery, moving on I was glad
Hair loss and sickness with chemo were rough
My attitude and tennis kept me so tough
Doctors and friends as a team kept me going
To the world, my smile and spirit was showing
When well, I'd play tennis between every round
Inspiring my friends with deep strength that I found
It's all about looking one day at a time
Onward and upward life then does climb
Genetics explained these mutations were rare
That made me high risk despite all my care
Advised more surgery for my safe moving on
Hysterectomy and more nodes to keep it all gone
At last there was good news, that it was all clear
So we had a grand party to close off the year
Inviting all those who helped on the way

Reminding them of how we now look at each day
Not to waste time in worry or hate
But to look at all good things before it's too late
We never can tell how our life will unfold
So rejoice for today, don't wait to get old

Courage

What is courage?
I thought it was when a stranger risked his life
To save a victim from certain tragedy
Or, is it the will to persevere
Through treating a deadly disease
And fight with deepest strength
Fatigue that is consuming
Pain that invades all thinking
Heartache of watching family suffer
Losing your identity
To become a patient
And find the power
To climb the mountain and reach the top
To enter uncertainty
To embrace the unfamiliar
That is courage.

Peace

Peace is:
To feel the inner calmness when anguish has stopped
To see those with huge burdens who surrender to grace
The resolution of pain when it was so severe
The acceptance of imperfection in yourself
Knowing the warmth of your family
Having friends who are always there
Realizing how much you are loved
To see the beauty and good in everything
The satisfaction of not needing any more than you have
Because no one could want more than life itself
Being able to smile in adversity
Because you have climbed a mountain
And will always know that you have that strength
Having faith in your journey
And believing your endurance and spirit
A place in your mind that you discover
When writing or creating, removing other thoughts
To accept the uncertainty of life because nothing in life is certain
Except now
Peace is in the present

Be A Yes Man

So out of my depth I had to say
"Yes," as so wounded in bed I lay
That was so hard, I'm always so strong
Facing a journey that was scary and long
So "yes" to the offers, that's the new you
And "yes" to the person I need to talk to
At first I thought I could manage alone
But insistence of help came over the phone
A listener came and opened my mind
Not knowing all the difficult things I would find
Acknowledging fear, allowing to cry
Adaptive tears for us to grow by
For now your hair and titles are gone
Loving yourself to learn to move on
I healed with a "yes" to writing and art
Accepting the change to make my new start
Push past your safe zone to get through the fight
Say "yes" when it's hard will prove you right

My Path

Life may not go where a path is made, go instead where there is no path and blaze a trail.

Art Therapy Nov 2010

We were instructed to paint a beautiful path. I envisioned a perfect fall day in the woods. We were then told to rip the watercolour painting into pieces, representing the chaos that ripped apart our perfect life. The torn, tattered pieces were then reassembled and remounted onto construction paper. A new path was painted through the ripped picture – how symbolic.

That path was my life. It was perfect – a wonderful husband, two wonderful children, a house, a career that I had always wanted and worked so terribly hard to achieve, so hard that it hurt sometimes.

It all was broken with one phone call. Everything changed. I couldn't bear it – it felt so uncertain, scary and controlling. All my plans and future path were erased. It made me feel so weak and helpless. I was angry to people comparing me to their path. Just because they had the same disease did not mean it was the same situation, extent, pathology or surgery. I hated the judgement, yet I did not want silence. I needed so much reassurance that a new path would appear since it felt like the edge of a cliff in the mist and I could not see ahead.

My new path is reappearing and it is different, just like the reassembled painting. A lot of good has come along the new path because I have embraced it. I still think that the end of the path is not clear and may not be for a while but I am going to keep looking at the beautiful trees and love the journey. I will rest on the way and may need help to find my way again but I am willing to follow it, not knowing where it is going now, confident that it is a good path.

Some people could not tear their painting. It was very hard to tear the beautiful picture but that helped me identify the pain that fractured through my life. Now I look at it differently.

The Mask

I knew I needed to find an avenue of help but was not a willing participant for group therapy. I had forgotten to cross my name off the art therapy list in my rush out of the cancer environment. When I was called for the class, I was assured complete anonymity – I did not even need to write my name for the group, that was the beauty of art. That seemed safe. So that was my approach for the first three classes.

My art therapy teacher explained that we must enter the room with an open heart and no preconceived ideas. To break down the control, art therapy was often done with the non-dominant hand or lines made with our eyes closed to separate the controlling part of our brain and let the emotion flow onto the paper or other media. We were told to allow the medium to "speak to you." This may mean watercolour paints, pastels or, this day I chose to throw a lump of clay.

The beautiful thing about clay is that it is changeable. I moulded the soft clay to a face shape and could change the expression from happy to sad and back.

I sat back to look at the final product and, as usual, to let the group know why this piece felt right today. As I looked at it I realized a very profound thing – I was hiding behind that mask, still scared to share and nobody knew my real story or who I was.

That was my turning point. That was my breakthrough day of risking authenticity and vulnerability – being judged as a doctor and a patient. I was supposed to be in control but now I was weak and it was terrifying. That is what I shared and never looked back.

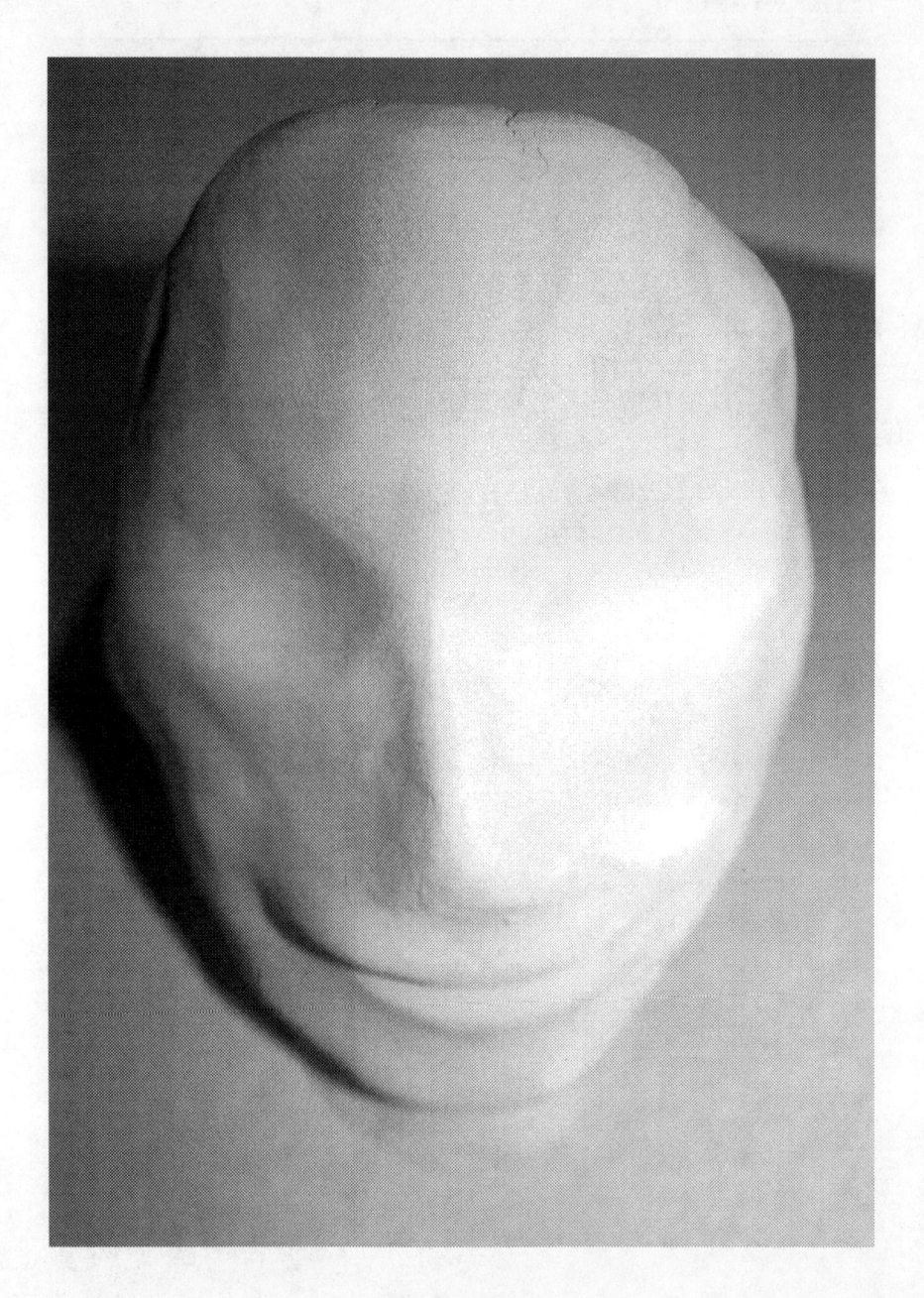

The Mask

Footprints In The Sand

Art Therapy November 2010 – One Step at a Time.

This was a piece I did in art therapy. It was one of those anxious, distressing days, realizing the guilt and caregiver burdens that cancer brings. I looked down at my feet to remember that you can only get through this one step at a time. I remembered the beach we walked upon just before my diagnosis and the long canvas "spoke" to me.

It was months later that I came across the attached verse, only to realize that in that difficult moment, I had already painted the picture that belonged to this!

A man in his dreams met his God.

He saw his life set out before him as footprints on a beach.

Sometimes there was one set of footprints in the sand and sometimes two.

He noticed that there was only one set of footprints in the hardest and most painful times in his life.

Angry that he had been abandoned in these toughest times, he asked the spirit why he was left alone in such challenging times in his life,

His God replied:

When there were only one set of footprints, my child; that's when I carried you.

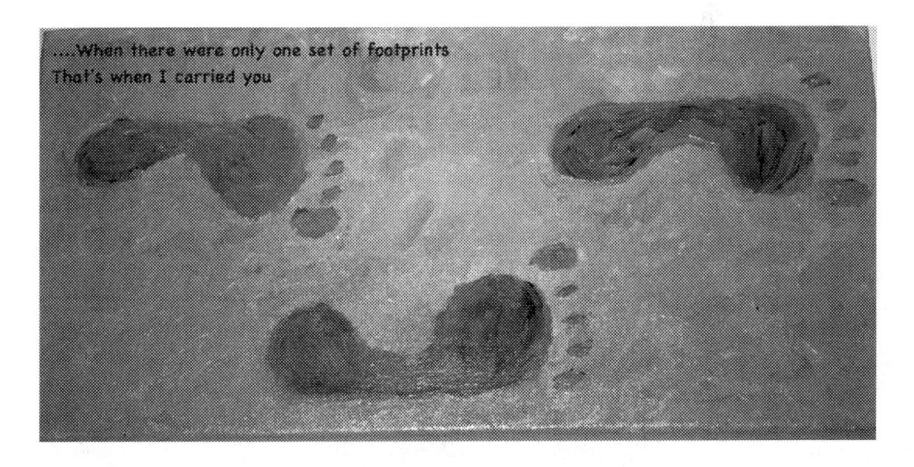

What Has Cancer Taught Me?

Who am I to be given this burden?
What is this silent and sinister disease?
How can it hurt so many yet empower so many more?
Why does it take so much away yet give back even greater?
Where am I going on this new path?

I have discovered great gifts to document this journey
I have found the inner strength of a warrior
I have been empowered to do great things and not be afraid
I have learned to enjoy every moment and see the good in everything
I have found a spiritual self that I did not know before
I have realized how special my friends and family are
I am a doctor and a patient – an experience to be used
I love life more than ever and see how precious and fragile it is

Cancer is a lesson for a selected few
A test of our endurance and faith
To believe in ourselves when drowning in results
And prevail with resilience and radiance
To inspire many and for those to inspire many more.

The Light And The Shadow

I always said cancer's shadow is there
A risk in my mind that I try not to share
Then it was clear, how bright was the light
That shone on my path with strength from the fight
It not only brightened my spirit to be
The light was so strong that it helped others see
That light can be found, just look for the glow
And doors will then open and through them I go
And so as the history stays on my file
I wish I could add how much I now smile
Not focus on shadows but thrive in bright sun
Filling life with adventure has now just begun.

> Light can be found, just look for the glow
> And doors will then open and through them I go

Light and Shadow

This is a negative painting where the dark trees are not painted; they are simply what remain by painting the background. It is about thinking differently.

Trust Is The Opposite Of Fear

As I put together my scrapbooking this week of endless lovely cards and stories of my journey from last year, it takes me back to intensely feeling what it was like – a sensation that is not all good. As a doctor, I am analyzing every twinge, knowing too much and trying to push those thoughts away. It was recently that I wrote down that Trust is the Opposite of Fear. If I could take every time that I worry and convert that into trusting my team, my anxiety drops significantly. I am not afraid to call at a persistent complaint and saying these words in my head help me to move the anxiety out of my head to someone else's decision, which feels so much better. I trust in a lot of people now – my doctors, my friends, a spirit of faith, my family, and myself. I don't say that it will all be ok but that they will be there for me, making decisions in my best interest and always trusting – that is the best I could ever ask for. Cleaning my mind out of these thoughts unloads decisions allowing me to move on and love living, being sensible, proactive but controlling fear.

* * *

Trust

Trust is my peace, handing over my fear
The way I can live and keep my mind clear
When worries or tests enter my brain
It's trust in my team that grounds me again
As I give to my patients, I reflect on my care
What I have received, I heart-feltly share
Knowledge is painful, anxiety too
So trusting their judgement is what I must do
Hand over my worries, it's where my job ends
Trust in my team – good colleagues and friends.

Believe

Believe

Believe in your confidence
Believe that you can overcome more than you think
Believe that time heals wounds – physical and mental
Believe that hard work pays off
Believe that nothing in life is free except love and sunsets
Believe in a spirit that makes good things happen
Believe that love is real
Believe that you have special gifts
Believe that you can do it
Believe that attitude is part of your medicine
Believe that you have purpose
Believe that good things can happen
Believe in the strength of friends
Believe that family will be there to hold you up
Believe in quality not quantity
Believe in the power of the moment, no matter how long life is
Believe that you will make a difference to many
Believe in paying forward kindness

The Outsider

This is one of my favourite poems – perhaps because I want so much to help the world see what they are missing. You never notice until you nearly lose it all.

    I was inspired to write this poem, as I want the world to see that life is fragile. You don't know when cancer or adversity could blindside you on an ordinary day. The other side to cancer is that it teaches you to pause and look around and make someone's day happy because that moment will not come back. We don't know how many moments life will give us so don't waste any on being angry or upset. I want to touch the "Outsider" to make them see what we have learned yet not have to tread adversity to get a glimpse.

* * *

The Outsider

I see them in the line-ups, I see them in the cars
The ordinary people who cannot see my scars
They do not know the feeling of fighting just to live
No time to smile, say hello or compliment to give
It's all about the deadline or that last parking space
I wish they saw that they could be, the next to cancer face
It changes all that rushing and that you can do it all
Friends and family hold you up when cancer makes you fall
Some would just feel awkward and talk of other things
Others talk of outcomes which intolerably stings
It is not that I want normal or return to who I was
Cancer opened up my eyes to change from that because
I like the person who says hello and lets that car in lane
Or lets the person cross the road and even loves the rain
I don't need a medal to accomplish every goal
Just the beauty of the moment to love life to my soul
To some, my story grounds them and they see another view

But many think that cancer could never affect you
To take a moment, you can learn just how this may feel
Don't try to be demanding or speeding at the wheel
And be the kind who loves each day and helps so many needs
You'll be surprised at who you are and where this attitude leads
The outsider's not protected from what tomorrow has in store
Break down that shell and learn from me that life's worth pausing for.

SECTION 2

Support

Positive Thinking Card 2

More Things to Remember

One day at a time. **Everyone has a story.** Allow more time. Inspire. Destiny. Every day is a special day – never take it for granted. Read. Push yourself – it feels great. You have great gifts – share them. Don't forget your family – they are amazing. Be a "yes man". Share the joy of life. Write. **Step beyond your comfort zone – you'll be proud of yourself.** Love the skin you are in – don't be jealous. Rest and take in the moment. Life is what you make it. Don't say words that you will regret. Say sorry. Say thank you. Create. Don't compare. Take the time to visit. Priorities. Be grateful. Deal with something that bothers you. Don't blame others. Don't expect others to understand how you feel. **Some people say the wrong thing – don't be angry.** Positive attitude. Friends are always there. Change things that are negative. Strength and courage prevail. Perseverance. Time heals. Believe in yourself. **Love myself as I am.** Remember your spiritual side.

There was a theme in this thinking card. I was angry. I did not want other people telling me their story. "Don't expect others to understand how you feel." There were the inappropriate comments and then some people were afraid of saying anything. "Some people say the wrong thing, don't be angry," helped me understand this. I could repeat this and it would calm my emotional reaction. Sometimes, I would hit a tennis ball so hard and give it all my deepest energy between chemo rounds that I felt lightheaded and had to sit to rest. I was exhausted but the catharsis felt amazing. It took me to a world where I wasn't a patient – "Push yourself, it feels great," came from that moment. Then we must remember that everything that was taken away will come back. Learning to "love myself as I am," was useful to keep reciting. I could not change anything except my thinking so this card helps me do just that.

These thinking cards contained simple words that stuck in my mind and the phrases would recite themselves when a situation arose, helping me see it differently.

Support

Last year's fear really reset my boundaries. Layers and layers of bad news made me so fragile and rebuilding this type of resilience has been hard. Pushing myself to uncomfortable boundaries is not easy – it is support that makes it possible. It helps me to take strong steps forward.

A patient asked me if they were going to die. It was not the first time I had answered that question but this time I felt the strength of support I could give. Now I want to be part of that team for other people. It may be as a doctor or a friend, a colleague or a family member, but that purpose is one of life's greatest rewards.

* * *

Support

Do you know of a fear where the world all stands still
It all seems surreal, I can't be this ill
And nights when those demons, dance in your head
Replaying the news of what doctors said
Though this is your race, a crowd cheers you on
And picks you back up when the road seems too long
Your team by your side gives you more strength to fight
Pull you out of the holes and into the light
It's trusting that team who'll always be there
The most precious gift is the time that they share

*Though this is your race, a crowd cheers you on
And picks you back up when the road seems too long*

"I'm Strong" – Art Therapy 2010:

We were told to do two comparison drawings: "I'm strong" and "I'm Fragile."

"I'm Strong," is about all those people cheering you on to give you strength. Cancer is your journey alone but I imagined a marathon race: you are tired, exhausted and so weak but look behind the ropes to all those people cheering you on with energy and encouragement. You just could not do it without them.

"I'm fragile," was drawn as a cracked egg surrounded by bombarding rocks. It is difficult to protect yourself from so much bad news but important to acknowledge these inner wounds that will heal with time and trust.

The Pyramid of Support

There was a story – A girl was upset with her life – that things were hard and unfair. Her father wanted to show her the meaning behind adversity…

He put 3 pots on the stove:

> In the first, he put a carrot
> In the second, he broke an egg
> In the third, he put ground coffee

After some time, he turned off the stove:

He then explained how differently each one reacted to the heat – the carrot went in hard but softened, the egg became hard and the coffee beans actually changed the water.
"When you confront adversity, which one will you be?" he asked. The carrot starts out strong but wilts under pressure, the egg becomes hardened with stress, or will you be the coffee bean that uses adverse conditions to change the ordinary water to something different, special and unique that pleases many people?
I like to look at cancer as a changing road in life. You can choose to look at the negative and be hardened by it or as a springboard to helping other people notice what they take for granted every day, never thinking how beautiful ordinary things are, never noticing the miracles of nature as they focus on deadlines and agendas. We can change this thinking – the positive side of cancer that I always focus on and open other people's eyes to our new vision.
I describe to people my Pyramid of Support. If I can inspire some people, to help them see life differently and how to access the tools to deal with adversity, then when they meet adversity themselves, as a friend, colleague or relative faces cancer or a devastating illness, they too pass on the tools from what they have learned. The pyramid of support becomes enormous. One touches hundreds who can touch dozens more. That is what this is all about – a pyramid of people reaching out with tools to help.

You will be the listening ears, knowing how to be there without needing a reason, being real and seeing that person as whom they are, not as a disease.

If a friend sees me and says, your name came up as I offered tips to my friend; that means the pyramid is working.

It is not about one person making a difference to many, it is about making a difference to one person at a time and then they pass it on to so many more
 – I hope the pyramid keeps growing and growing.

Look In Your Village

We are programmed to need attachment – a fundamental human need. It is the single most important factor for mental wellness. With a history of well-cultivated attachment, when loss happens, whether the loss of a loved one or severe trauma or illness, it is the people around us that predict our success. It is about the union and reunion – the sense of caring as we receive empathy and validation of our weakness and vulnerability. Those people that are always there, no need to pretend, they just understand. Family, friends, coworkers, neighbours, teams – that's our village.

When I was going through my journey I had some very important "rocks" to lean on, solid and true – each one had a role. When my treatment finished, a friend asked me to help her friend. She told me a remarkable observation though – she said that it was so good to have me but that she would be her "rock" – a role that she had observed was just as important. Yes there are so many roles in support, often overlooked, but it is about mobilizing "your village" when cancer strikes.

Crying is important for our nervous system – it is a way of releasing stressors. In grief it is expected to release those emotions, have a shoulder to lean on and soak the tears. Never think for a moment that the loss of who you were is small – the innocence of seeing life as always in front of us, young and endless is recalibrated, the invincibility knocked crashing down and pushing past fears now creates new horizons. It is important to release these stressors, crying and grieving what has been lost is normal and needed in order to venture forwards and grow. This is where the rock of stability is needed – your village of support.

I had great fear of sharing with others that had been through cancer during my treatment. My struggle could only include me at the time. I couldn't take someone telling me what to eat to stop cancer coming back when I knew the science behind this disease. Only afterwards did I come up for breath and realize there was grace to be learned from amazing people in handling this massive emotional burden. My village expanded to Wellspring and a connection on-line to fellow bloggers – positive people, all with different roads – these people were not rocks but wings to lighten the burden, help me to fly again and embrace uncertainty without fear because it now looks like adventure instead.

So I now nurture my village – I just didn't see it before:
Find your village
Notice your village
Accept help
Priorities
Share your burdens
Cry and hurt
Validate feelings
Acknowledge losses
Find your wings to adventure again
Pay forwards
Nurture your village…

SECTION 3

Back To Work

Positive Thinking Card 3

> ### Things to Remember Moving On
>
> Sleep on it – its better in the morning. Remember your new path. You got through last year – you can get through anything. Inspire. Book coffee with a friend. Visit. Take a moment to call – it is worth a thousand thoughts. Healing some wounds takes 6 weeks – others way longer. **Go beyond your comfort zone- you'll be proud of yourself.** Take more time. Give yourself permission to play. Book art time. Book reading time. Play tennis. **Go to that place in your head where time stands still.** Balance. **Make things happen – they don't always fall in your lap.** Make to do lists. Write. Forgive yourself. You are not perfect- don't expect perfect. **Only the healthy me is helpful.** Lead with your heart. You are rare. Be patient of your healing. Do what you can do. Speak out to relieve the burden. **Don't look back unless to gain wisdom.** Fear is part of me but lives quietly in peace. Choose to be happy. All you can do is always enough. Focus on positives. Trust yourself. Find your confidence – dig deep sometimes.

Going back to work has its own set of worries but I live by, "Only the healthy me is helpful." This keeps me giving as much of myself as I can while watching my own health doesn't suffer. When going outside your comfort zone feels a bit tough, go just an inch more and you'll be proud of yourself. Don't forget to go to that place in your head that you love – swim, create, exercise – it is healthy and we only thrive on balance.

What is it like back at work? Exciting to cross that barrier from sickness to wellness. Determined to be seen as the warrior, not the victim. I am the one who slayed the cancer dragon. That is when people want to be around you and find out how you did it. I am conscious of not draining friends of their energy, not dragging them down, being an inspiration of energy, not absorbing their energy; afraid that will turn them off. It is a tough road. Friends can go home and renew energy but family cannot. I cannot drag them down too. They were already doing twice the work with groceries, especially my husband. The kids wanted it to be over, to believe that it was all in the past. The duration of this recovery is trying on my close family and staying strong for them is important. Sometimes my emotions are not as real around them since they do not want to hear that I hurt any more.

At first I started work on half days only. No activities were planned in the afternoons. Of course, patients were ecstatic to see me, which gave me motivation and excitement. My colleagues were so happy too. It was hard to believe that I could go through all that and come back. But my mind got so tired. It felt like I had just written a qualifying exam each day with headaches of concentration and not an ounce of energy left. After four weeks of half days in addition to all the usual mother duties, hospital and nursing home rounds and on-call weekends, I realized my limitations. It was so humbling to realize that though I could play some tennis, my mind was struggling with multitasking and getting through the rapid assessments, paperwork, decision-making, phone calls and the pace that my job required.

I am so fortunate to be able to preach my message of living life to its fullest every day and be grateful for every moment. I remind people how growing old is a privilege that we don't all have. It is a beautiful thing. I remind them how aching side effects of drugs mean that they are doing their job at stopping disease, just like mine. It is the price of keeping cancer away.

My excitement to be back resembles the day that I got into medical school after all those years of hard work. It is a privilege to be able to come back to this and for so many people to trust in me when I doubted my own ability to return. I now notice that I radiate positive energy at work and it is contagious.

My Team

Have you ever known a family 1000 people strong
Who wait for my return the whole treatment year long
Then bring me gifts of happiness on my office day
And thanks and hugs on my return that the cancer is away
Never would you know this love without such tragic pain
That tears of caring fill their eyes that this won't come again
We all have courage inside ourselves, more than you will know
Sharing this empowers them; this is what I show
My colleagues keep supporting me as tiredness makes me slow
I'm driven by excitement but with balance I must go
The love for life is radiant and infectious in my team
Enjoying every moment I laugh and hug and gleam
I've been given back my life that I worked so hard to find
The multitasking challenges for my anxious chemo mind
Remember when you're running late or patients want you more
That all these people love you and that's worth fighting for
You're not just a number, an interesting case
You are the link in a great team, a fighter and kind face
You understand how fear is real, to live each day with love
You may have paths that seem unclear but together we rise above.

Making A Difference

I want to teach the world to sing
And thank each day for everything
There those who want to blame
And dwell on what is not the same
Instead reach out with what is new
Use adversity to strengthen you
But only can compassion come
If you have healed from what has gone
Don't be angry at who you're not
Or what you've lost or haven't got
Find that spirit to light your way
Moving forwards to heal each day
Love your scars and don't look back
Look at what you have, not what you lack
Make a difference to the person you meet
Then they do the same to each person they greet
And soon you make changes you never would know
Imagine how far such this spirit could go.

A Hospital Journey

For 15 years I took those calls
I saw my patients and walked those halls
Any emergency, they were all there
My surgeon, nurses, you know who care
Never could it cross my mind
That I'd fight for life of a different kind
I gave them trust as their faces told
Through cancer surgeries, my hand they'd hold
The news got worse and operate more
Too many times on that surgical floor
Nurses listened through fragile tears
And helped me through such difficult fears
Hearing the story in the pain of night
Attitude to wins, stay with the fight
A patient with cancer, it shadows me still
A passion to show what its like when so ill
As a doctor, my heart now feels their pain
And helps them to realize their strength again
Support and you'll see the feeling to give
Is better than anything, purpose to live
To change a journey doesn't take much
Time to listen is a heart you'll touch.

SECTION 4

Motivation

Positive Thinking Card 4

> **No Excuses**
>
> No Excuses. There's always a way. **Choose to be happy.** Pay forward kindness. Balance. Believe in yourself. Speak with your actions – be a role model. Save thank you cards – know that you are loved. Celebrate everyday. Don't complain – step up to the plate. Focus on the comeback one step at a time – that's life. **Don't be afraid of embarrassment – you'll miss the chance of success. When life throws you curve balls – learn to hit them back.** No need for medals – fulfillment comes from within. Miracles are not always what you wish for – they may be right in front of you. Give compliments. Give a card – because. Paint sunflowers. Wear your heart on your sleeve – believe in yourself. Think of everything you love. **If you focus on the negative, you miss the thousand positive things that can happen.** Take educated risks. **Looking after everyone includes yourself. Trust is the opposite of fear.** Make a difference. **Be the one.** Make someone's day. Exercise cleanses the chaos. Exercise the mind- keep learning. Believe strengths are bigger than weaknesses. Stay grounded. Wear your spirit, not your wig.

When you fall down 10 times you must get up 11 times without excuses but with the strength of an army of friends. The power of all those great people gives us confidence.

On a celebratory snowboarding trip, just six weeks back at work, I broke my shoulder – the same one as my axillary dissection. Immobilized, it all seized up again. The nausea and pain were so tiring, which gave me doubts of recovery. Everything hurt again. I finally took up my tennis racquet again, held on tighter to the waterski handle, reached for that attitude and put the pain aside. "No Excuses." "There's always a way." That is how Positive Thinking Card 4 was born.

As my little tufts of hair sprouted, I decided that I was not going to wear my scarf at the gym. It took several minutes to leave the change room with an almost naked head, but was met with compliments from friends. So I stated, "I was wearing my spirit, not my wig now." It gave me pride to say those words and I held onto that phrase in moments of discomfort with my bare image in the gym mirror. Yes, it is really uncomfortable to see that steroid face with no hair in the gym mirror next to the pretty blonde ponytails but I would say the words loud in my head and little did I know that I was inspiring others – a fact that later, many people revealed to me.

Paint sunflowers

No Excuses

I could have blamed the sideways wind, the damp court, the cold weather on my aching joints when I was not connecting with the ball but what would that prove – no excuses I say to myself. If I blame it on something else, how can I expect to overcome these adversities? Playing tennis outside is a different game – it takes working it out to do better.

It takes me back to my chemo rounds when I would turn up on day 10-20 post-infusion to hit. Yes, day 20, look out, I was on high dose steroids – not accurate but whacking the ball on sleep deprived energy boost. If I allowed myself to blame my weakness on the score, I would always lose, so, "No Excuses" was my mantra. Of course, we have to recognize our limitations – don't make an impossible goal, only one that is incremental, reachable, achievable, within your capabilities but just a little up the challenging scale.

On several occasions, people explained that they had been away on holiday so may not hit as well then quickly realized what they were saying as they played this attitude. Never start the game with forgiveness or excuses – it is about possible. Nothing else. Figure out the solution and try again otherwise you've given yourself permission not to try so hard.

It all comes down to our "Locus of Control." Internal Locus of Control says that your inner attitude controls your success – that if it is not working then you have to figure it out to make it happen. An "External Locus of Control" suggests that the outcome is due to external factors – that life circumstances, my surgeries or cancer treatment, the weather, my racquet, what you eat, other people are the reason for your lack of success. Sometimes these factors are there but it is clear that the Internal Locus of Control is needed for self-satisfaction and achievement of our goals within our reachable levels, whatever that may be.

It applies to life – who said it was easy? But we don't have to see failure as a stopping point, only a learning point to figure it out and try again. It may not be about things turning out the way you planned but trying it differently or in a new direction to create success.

So I made this poem, not because I can get it all right. It is really about what I try to teach myself to remember – to redirect my thinking. Poems have a cadence that allows the phrases to ring in my head when I am late or trying to explain why I am not winning. If I can try and change this attitude instead of accepting it, I will improve and change – we are humble to that.

* * *

No Excuses

I just need possible, nothing to blame
Don't give excuses that things aren't the same
Failure's a lesson; now figure it out
Notice your thoughts and what it's about
Attitude rules, not limitations
No excuses will give new expectations
When it hurts or you're tired think of success
Try your best and go further, don't settle for less
Find the good not the bad; be confident, it shows
Be determined; don't give up, no excuses I chose
Say what you mean, keep to your word
Don't overschedule, no excuses you heard
Decide and stick with it one step at a time
No excuses is how, up mountains you climb
Write it down, plan ahead, no excuse, don't be late
Respect other schedules; don't make them wait
Don't make your challenge too big or too small
And forgive yourself if you don't reach it but fall
Just pick yourself up, No excuses to know
We learn to get better, and that's how we grow.

It is not about doing it all, just making reachable challenges and figuring it out when it doesn't work to come back and try again – No Excuses.

Motivation Poem

If you think you can't do it, you won't
If you think you'll lose, you already have
If you don't set your dreams at the top, you'll never reach them
If you are defeated by small things, they have weakened you
If you keep taking the short way you will loose stamina
Comparison is rarely constructive
If you don't listen to change, you can't expect to improve
Success is a state of mind
Pride in accomplishments is the motivation
Strengths come from exposing weaknesses
Friends never give up on you so neither should you
Bravery is not measured by the thickness of your armour
But the size of your heart within
Endurance is not the size of your muscle
But the tenacity to hold on
The smartest minds are those who figure it our when it seems impossible
Not the top of the class
Winning is not all talent, it is the undivided desire to achieve it
And the confidence to believe it
Life's challenges are not won by the biggest or fastest man
But by the person who thinks he can.

ABCs Of Moving On

Attitude – You can make a difference, you can find a way, play the cards you are dealt. Choose to be happy – it is the same effort
Believe – Believe in yourself – that you have more strength and perseverance than you realized.
Change – You have more control than you think – have the strength to change things that don't work, don't look back unless to gain wisdom
Dress up – It says you care. The will to **do**; the soul to **dare**
Enough – All you can do is always enough
Family – Remember your family, they're amazing. You are loved more than you ever realized.
Grounding – It's all relative – you got through cancer, you can get through anything. Vitamin G
Heal – Sleep on it – its better in the morning. Heal yourself mentally too – chemo fog is real. Be patient of your healing. Only the "healthy me" is helpful.
Inspire – Show your inner strength and be proud of how far you have come. To inspire is not to compare.
Job – Love your job – do what makes you come alive
Know – know your limits. Know you are loved
Laugh – Laugh at how trivial some problems seem now. Laugh at yourself. Laugh at mistakes
Make – Make things happen, they don't always fall in your lap. Make to do lists. Make pictures.
Never – Never take each day for granted. No complaints – take a pill
One – One day at a time, live in the present. You are one of a kind – A diagnosis unites us, our paths all different, don't compare.
Positive thinking – Cancer has awakened the beauty in everything and everyone. Positive thinking does not wear others down, it attracts them.
Queen of Courage – Strength, perseverance and courage prevail.
Quiet time – restore
Remember – Never to forget how much can be taken away. Resilience is post-traumatic growth

Spirit – It shines brighter than any accessory. Smile – you look better

Tennis – Play tennis – it takes you to that place in your head where time stands still. Feel the sweat, push yourself, it feels great.

Tenacity – hold on to that rope – want it, you will make it – stay the course, even when it is rough

Understand – don't expect others to understand how you feel. Some people say the wrong thing, don't be angry

Visit – take time to visit friends and family. Keep priorities clear. Call – it's worth a thousand thoughts

Write – When it upsets you write it down, it works

No eX**cuses** – there's always a way, e**X**ercise, don't e**X**pect perfect – imperfect is the new perfect

Yes – Be a "yes" man. Say yes to more than you want to, you'll be surprised at the results

Zone – Go beyond your comfort zone; you'll be proud of yourself

Energy

One day I looked at my living room and realized that it was the "old me" – it was dreary and conservative with old copies of art in traditional frames. I bought a pot of beautiful blue/gray paint and transformed my rooms. Yes, I did it – I love the transformation that a simple pot of paint makes. The walls also covered in inspirational photos of bridges to distant places, sunlight through forests and fresh feelings to surround me in the new feelings of life that I have. Not to stop there, I took another pot of paint to another dreary room and made the sunlight flood the walls in new soft colours.

I can look at a project now with new eyes – more energy than I have had for 2 years. I struggled through last year with more surgeries and tragic death of my mother in law. I had no idea how little energy I had until I got it back. I remember feeling that driving was exhausting and a project insurmountable, but I got things done, no more. Wow, how different it looks with energy again. It is humbling to remember that exhaustion and grateful to feel life now. I feel like I have to fit it all in.

I am playing tennis with strength and endurance now – my first league match on Saturday since my broken wrist – a very tiring rehab of pain, stiffness and determination. I am back – attitude, strength and energy – what a gift never to take for granted.

* * *

Energy

What does it look like, how does it feel
Energy, endurance after I heal
One step was so hard but now so much more
To play tennis and win like never before
It's the fire of persistence, the spirit of dance
Exciting new projects with life's second chance
That out of the weakness, I now thrive
Energy and excitement that I'm alive

A story through dark and now to the light
To remind others of that will to fight
Determined, push forwards, now to be
Not empty or weak but a charged battery
It's hard to find balance, just ask me to play
I cannot say no since I live for today
My spirit is bright and energy too
A positive spirit radiates through
People now comment that I look well
I truly believe that – how much they can tell
I struggled uphill for such a long time
With winds and storms that battered my climb
Now a privilege to feel sore muscles ache
Not wounded or broken but living I'll take
Fulfilled with my day, so happy to be
Looking at tasks with restored energy

It's Not Just About Winning

As we sat after a round robin doubles tennis yesterday and asked each other – Why do we love tennis? It is clear that in this countdown to New Years Resolutions, exercise is always top of the list. I see the over packed parking lot in Jan and the scurry in the change room as people cannot remember their lock combinations and wonder why in two months the rush will be over and same ones remain. How can we change that? Exercise is as good as a drug but it is much harder work. It has been proven that it decreases risk of cancer, diabetes and heart disease and evidence-based studies show it improves mood, improves stamina and I think there is a component of mental determination that comes from fighting through exhaustion that can serve us well in our emotional challenges. So exercise is on my list too and my hand arthritis is really challenging but keeping the list reminds me. Hard work needs motivation:

The list came pouring out of my head.
Comrades – show up because they came out to play with you
Book exercise – no excuses when it is booked
Try – try your best, you will keep getting better
Clear mental chaos – you can't hit the ball if there are other thoughts in your mind
Mathematical challenge – the ball doesn't just go back and forth – it is not just a lucky hit or miss – there is set up and strategy, your mind recalculating and adjusting
Fitness – singles is an exhausting game: – cross train with purpose – weights, elliptical and pilates – that's the only way not to get injured
Friends – devoted, a family of friends – a social sport
Self-esteem – we all need to feel important, being in a sport where you matter is a great feeling.
Confidence – challenge yourself – you may be surprised if you work out how to get a point and win. Celebrate even the smallest successes
Perseverance – you have to want it to push yourself hard – that is infectious

Go there – working out in the presence of others has so many benefits. You stay longer, are less distracted by other tasks and social connections are so important. The readiness to exercise is booked and reserved when you go.

Happiness – all those endorphins – Dopamine, Serotonin, Norepinephrine serve you well when you get home and deal with kids

Catharsis – whack out your frustrations, leave them on the court – that is a great feeling!

Attitude – know that even when the chips are down, that you are not winning, it is always one point at a time – just focus in front of you. It keeps you coming back with fighting attitude because you have to believe you can do it.

Dedication – be there. Period. Keep to your word – it is your reputation, then you are invited back

Be humble – there's always more to learn – keep practicing.

Time – there's always someone who will play in those crazy hours after work, whenever you can grab an hour – find the time, you work it in when it is booked

Work out to great music – "spirit run" is the playlist on my shuffle. Sweat!

Give back – get fit and give back – at first I walked then I realized I could run – Run for the Cure, Terry Fox, Hospital fundraisers – not too far, stay in your fitness category, it is not about winning, it is about doing.

Staying in the moment – just for a moment, nothing else matters – the phone, the pager, the schedule. Just now is a sweet place.

Supportive family – be a role model and do exercise together – share the enthusiasm, it's infectious.

Priorities – make it one – I am grumpy without my dose of exercise.

Treat yourself – I have fancy soaps for the after-exercise shower – that's worth it.

Do what you love, love what you do – that includes exercise.

Grateful – these are the people who stand by you when cancer strikes and celebrate new life when treatment ends, see you beyond a scarf and believe you will play again after every chemo round….

Let's keep exercise on our list.

Lessons From Snowboarding

When I can break down fear into one mogul at a time, it becomes a skill that I can look at. This one is too big for me but maybe there are a few lessons from life that apply.

Do something that scares you – you'll be proud of yourself
Have a winning attitude
When you fall down 9 times, get up 10 times
Have a good leader – gives you confidence to try harder things
Visualize your path – just in front of you, that's all you need
Be offensive to the mountain – don't let it win
Balance Keep your arms out and let your hips do the turning
Go around obstacles
Take your own time
Share the fun times
Take breaks. Rest when you're tired
Sleep well
Hydrate
A mountain of moguls are less scary, one bump at a time
Listen to the beauty of silence
Grunt to get that last bit of energy when exhausted
Laugh together
Laugh at mistakes
If you don't fall sometimes, you're not trying hard enough
Success feels awesome- remember that feeling
There's always more to learn
You're never too old to learn new things
Recalibrate fear
Go outside your comfort zone
Put your trust in good hands – especially at 124.7 km/hr on a bobsled
Know your limits
Don't quit
When you are stuck in a tree hole, think of a solution

Everyone has a story – not just you
Take the last lift to the top
Set a goal
Fresh tracks
Play till the sun goes down
Look back up the hill at what you've accomplished – its quite remarkable
The only way to the bottom is one turn after the next – that's the power of determination
Self check fatigue
Bruises are part of improving
Turn on your second engine when it seems so hard.

No Should-ing Allowed

Should means you can but you haven't
Should allows room for avoidance
Should doesn't make decisions
Should has intention without momentum
Should pleases others more than you
Should means your goal is too big to achieve
Don't should it – book it
Shoulds are never scheduled
Don't be a should-er, be a Do-er

I hear it all the time, "you are right, I should book that, should do that, should exercise". No should-ing allowed is how I try to look at life now and try and help people including myself go from should to Do... is called stages of change. Five stages of change exist to categorize our goals.

If you sit in the phrase "I just can't do that because..." You are in PRECONTEMPLATON – denial or seemingly impossible undertaking that is beyond achievement in your mind. You may feel that you are a victim in that position and it is up to others but this is where should-ing is out and doing is in. We must always find our internal locus of control – believe that you can do it, even when it is hard – That's your starting point.

So now I have got you thinking.... This is where the should-ers come in. Thinking about it, CONTEMPLATION – should do it but it still seems hard so you have to look into a way of making it possible. Should-ers look at the barriers to change – time, expense, fear. It may be at this point that you reassess the size of your goal to make it more possible – this is the key – make your goal achievable and reachable even if it is really small.

Are you ready for ACTION? Out of should-ing to Do-ing! Keep to the plan; make the plan small and reachable. If it is too much, make it smaller. This is the point where we must be totally honest with ourselves. Sneaking a snack only hurts you. This is a goal for you only.

MAINTENANCE – lets make this real. If you think that you can juice your diet or spend two hours preparing the most wholesome organic meal every day – you are pretty likely to fail maintenance. This is a lifetime level. It has to fit in to everyday life always. People are full of good intentions at getting up at 5 am to exercise but if you cant sustain that then half an hour at lunchtime is going to give you more success in the long run. You cant cut out carbs for the rest of your life so try a formula bound for long term appeal – permission to be real or we are doomed to fail or RELAPSE.

So when someone says, "we should get together for coffee," surprise that person with the "shoulds are out" rule and book it. Even if you change it, we become Do-ers.

SO I ALWAYS REMEMBER:

The past is behind you except to learn from it
Make a goal that is reachable
Decide to say yes
No shoulds allowed.

The Power Of Great Feelings

When you live in the moment, it's that awesome feeling – nail something hard, against the odds, with determination and drive that consumes your mind. It is that feeling that keeps you coming back. When things seem tough and the only way is forward, those feelings give you power and strength. When things don't work out right, those feelings remind you to try again. It is clear that endorphins produced in exercise, help to control pain – not only can exercise help but the memory of that power and good feeling is such great therapy too.

I remember after the axillary dissection, having extensive adhesions in my axilla. My husband called the scarring my "Bat Wing" as it webbed across my armpit. Intense physiotherapy required pulling apart the scarring. It was the only way to free up my arm to get my tennis serve again and reach for my front crawl swim stroke. As she pulled the tissue and nerves, my body sweated with pain and she would tell me to "imagine a good place and focus on good feelings." I would force my mind to go to a thrill zone of success – a moment of feeling great to take my mind off the pain as I concentrated on breathing.

So I imagine all those moments when my mind was in another zone: awesome moments that I still love so much – my mind takes a photo to always go there:

Nail that low percentage shot down the line in tennis – awesome
Coming back from behind to win
The moment you pull out of the water on a slalom waterski start
A glass of red wine at the water edge arriving at the cottage
Coffee in bed in the morning on the weekend
Riding up and down a big bank of snow on my snowboard
Dancing to great music – your soul in the zone
That wahoo moment of leaning back on your snowboard in the powder
Screaming on a roller coaster that is totally out of your comfort zone
Warmth of sun at the end of the day with a good book

Turning up the music in the car to that "Invincible" song and singing along
The noise of going so fast on a snowboard, holding control –
    because you have to
GO TO THAT PLACE IN YOUR HEAD – LET'S RIDE.

Don't Be Afraid to Try; Just Modify

At the end of the busy week, exercise is my reward. I remember when my body had so many insults to it from mastectomies to reconstructions, armpit node removals, chemo and hysterectomy, gallbladder, hernia and two broken arms in just two years. I could do so little but sit on a stationary bike and bit-by-bit I could do more. Now my wrists don't bend much and as we prepared for the class, it was noted that I was the person who had to modify the exercises. I was proud of my ability to be there, proud that it can be adapted around things that can get you down such as the fractures. Yoga and pilates I do on my elbows. I just need possible. We must be mindful of balance but, "push yourself – it feels great."

Fit some exercise into your day to feel those good endorphins and don't be afraid to try – just modify.

* * *

Don't Be Afraid to Try; Just Modify

Its not about perfect, it's the will to be there
Don't focus on skill or the fact you've no hair
You may not be fastest or have the best bike
Just be proud that you're doing something you like
It's all about you, don't compare to your friends
We all have limitations on which it depends
The will to turn up is now up to you
Strength from inside is what pushes through
Unique and resilient is what we can be
Praise and support is what you will see
Say yes and don't be afraid to try
There's always a way – just modify.

Positive Thinking

The word malignant was so hard to hear
From colleagues their words hurt, their hearts so sincere
I imagined me drowning in waves 10 feet high
Swimming for life, not pausing to cry
Positive thinking took all of my might
To coach myself through this difficult fight
Not to compare, find my new way,
Smile and write journals, live for each day
No excuses, play tennis, take pills for the pain
Notice your family and visit again
I know not to judge any person I see
Who knows what they face, it may be like me
Ask for help, don't be proud, that's the path to get well
Find a person to listen to all that you tell
A team of support to be by your side
Some for just laughing and some to confide
Remember my list and a positive phrase
Reminding me of those difficult days
It keeps me grounded not to forget
To balance my life and priorities set.
Cancer's a label I'll always wear
But to look at the positive is a gift I can share

Inner Strength – Find Your Greatness

There's a theory that if bad memory paths are recurrently used, like any neurologic connection, they become easier to access. In tennis we call it "muscle memory." If we practice that shot hundreds of times, it works better and better. Everyone knows this when they have to sit down to piano practice and run the fingers up and down the scales. We are told to learn new things; do Sudoku and crosswords to exercise our brain pathways too. Some pathways we do not want to wear down and exercise – acknowledging the unpleasant thought and redirecting your mind before feelings are connected to it. It requires us to "notice" our thoughts.

We must not stop living life, afraid of the future. Remembering how to live each day and finding inner strength to take a step at a time whether you are 29 or 99 years old is so important. Like athletes, our mind can be our strength to get through pain and difficulty when the road gets so tough, using "self talk" to find that winning attitude when the body wants to quit. We may all meet these hurdles in some way and tapping into that determination, recognizing we must do only what is right in front of us is a great lesson.

Inner Strength is a learned behaviour that we can perfect, just like an Olympian.
To acknowledge that we are allowed to be afraid; that is normal.
That all we need to see is what is in front of us right now.
Life only makes sense backwards; trust that you will see that some day.
We all have greatness inside us.

Inner Strength Poem

Life's like a storm that knocks you down
And tests your strength in case we drown
To ask our hearts if we are tough
To find a way when things get rough
When it's hard to find your feet
As waves knock hard to find defeat
With pain inside that some don't see
Determination's the key to adversity
Find your friends who can see those powers
That pull you through life's hardest hours
Like an athlete of strength, believe that you
Can climb great mountains in all you do
Trust in the present; embrace the now
Don't worry forward but show the world how
Your inner strength will keep you on track
It will only make sense when you look back

What I Would Put In My Awesome Day?

Emotion comes when it hurts so much. I remember lying there after so much recent surgery, the white blood cell stimulating injections aching the fresh wounds and joints to just breathe to the next minute, hoping that some pain medication would work. I could lie there and look at pictures on my phone to remember such good feelings and take my mind there. A form of mindfulness to wilfully transport our emotion to the place that feels better. And so the list of good thoughts and dreams fill my head instead:

Remember the small things; One day they will be big things:

Wake up when I am rested – at the cottage
Coffee in bed in the morning
A morning swim in the lake
Ride in a car with the roof down
Play tennis – singles
Read the newspaper with fresh French bread
Create something
Go out for dinner
Dress up and dance to great music
Meet inspiring people that remind you why you are here
Go shopping with a friend somewhere extravagant
Open some special wine
Laugh
Fresh towels in the morning
Fresh sheets
Smell of thanksgiving dinner on a cold day
Hot tub after skiing

What I Learned From Others

As we sat there in grief recalling so many happy memories, she told me which was the best waterproof mascara for crying. I thought about all the things I have learned – not the medical drugs or diseases but pearls of life. Among all the medical challenges are real people like me with stories and feelings and taking the time to feel that is the part that makes my job so different and rewarding.

And so I thought about the list:

Wear the best waterproof mascara for crying
Treat people like you want to be treated yourself
Bad things happen to good people – we will never understand this
Sleep is the answer to a lot of problems – get enough
A phone call is worth a thousand thoughts
Always apologize for being late
Don't prejudge
Don't look back unless to learn from it
A hug is a great thing
Admit to mistakes, no excuses
Be there for your parents
Understand your kids
Don't smoke
Wear sunscreen
Wear your seatbelt
Listen to your body
Get travel insurance
Exercise
Eat fibre
Be a role model
Don't procrastinate
Challenge your mind
Get vaccinated

Walk a dog
Never stop learning
Don't forget to say goodbye every day
Trust your instincts
Be decisive, make it happen, take charge
Be a good listener
Not all problems are physical
Know what poison ivy looks like
40% of happiness is how you think about it
See a dentist regularly
Denial leads to trouble
Trust
Contemplation is the beginning of change
You can never spoil a child with love
Remember how good reassurance feels – take the time
Open red wine on Friday night
Be real. Be yourself. Be there

GrrrAttitude

Life, for me, had all the balls in the air – every moment accounted for. Then, on an ordinary day in April, it stopped – I found a lump. It was cancer. Another lump on the other side – it was cancer too, then into the lymph node. My agenda collapsed: tennis league – delete all, work – delete all. I felt like hiding away after so much pain and surgeries to remove the cancers with a double mastectomy and more. Yes, I broke the same bad shoulder last year and yes, I broke the same wrist badly this year, but I know I can come back now. It is not about me, it is about all those people who had faith and patience to see you as who you are, not a patient, knowing that attitude prevails and maybe rubs off a bit too as we all realize that determination is the key ingredient in life with GrrrAttitude.

* * *

GrrrAttitude

How do we discover who we are
It takes a journey very far
It is not just the fear of loosing your life
There's a void in yourself, cut out by a knife
My title, my looks, I thought defined me
I discovered resilience I never would see
The strength of endurance, courage to smile
Despite all the hurt it took me a while
To learn that from bad, the good will arise
That from this experience, I will be wise
And help people see that if you believe in you
There's a life of purpose in all that you do.

Vitamin G Today

It was Dr. Ginty, then Dr. G, now it's Vitamin G! Everyone needs a daily dose of it – thinking differently. Remember all those good thoughts that make you realize how awesome life is and how incredibly devastating when you can't find your way out of the increasingly deep pit of bad results. It is about the second chance and realizing it, soaking it up immensely in case you ever lose it.

Someone smiled at you today
Someone thinks the world of you
Stars on a clear night – millions of them
Crisp new clothes
Smell of a newly bathed baby
Something you've been wanting just happened
You made brave decisions
You are empowered
You are an angel to someone
Flowers are beautiful
Rain is beautiful
You are stronger than you ever believed
You've profoundly impacted someone's life
Maybe even saved one. Knowingly or not
You matter. Deeply. Hugely
You have goals and dreams
Some of them have come true
Others are on their way
Positive people
Inspiring energy
Grace of experience
Loving yourself
Sunrises
Sunsets together
Warm fires

A home to come to
Someone brought you something because
You made a bad decision. Two. Hundred. And lived. Wiser
Get excited.
Dance
Worlds collide – look for the connections and embrace them
Purpose and passion
Kindness is a great cure
Post your love and strength in front of you daily
Coffee
Run, walk, smell, feel, hear, touch, appreciate
Hang in there when exhausted
Hair is great. Period.
You are powerful
You can change someone today
Don't use up today thinking about yesterday
Notice your mood
You light up the room
Love the present; you worry less
You are genuine
People trust you
You are wise
Understand and listen.
Apologize and switch roles for a minute
Friday
Cookie exchanges
Potlucks of cultural food
Some days you are the statue, others the pigeon – that's life
Being happy is Hot
Being Hot is menopause – its more amusing than distressing
When you can't change the situation, change how you think about it
Happiness is a state of mind
Red wine with good company
Long, hot showers
Keep learning
Rise to challenges

Breathe and take the next step forwards
Latin quotes
You are good enough – always
Worthy
Deserving
Determined
Imperfect is the new perfect
Vulnerability is what people are looking for
Jumping in the lake. Running jump.
Choice, your choice
Coffee with a friend. Again.
Appreciation
Kick out cancer thoughts
For every piece of bad news there is and equal and opposite force of
    good news
Look for the good
Love your work. Fulfillment.
Love the reason you work
Find peace in balance
Notice imbalance. Change it.
There is always a way – always
Compromise
Been through hell and made it through the other side. Share the spirit.
You changed someone and they changed many more. Because of you
Every grain of sand makes a beach
Someone wants to be like you
Dress to suit your mood
This will pass. This will pass. This will pass
Caterpillars turn into goo to become beautiful butterflies
You make a difference to someone's world. Every day.
Mutual respect
Christmas decorations
Tidying up
Painting a room to transform that feeling around you
Feel how you live. Live how you feel.
Crying is authentic. Don't hide it.

Be a shoulder
Hug – be the first one.
Happy people get fewer colds and more hugs
Make it happen. Be the one.
Notice when it is just right.
Aut inveniam viam aut faciam – I will either find a way or make one.
You are a winner
There are more minutes in a day than you think

Remarkable people do not just happen.

SECTION 5

Balance

Positive Thinking Card 5

> ### Words of Wisdom
>
> Trust your intuition. Where there's a will, there's a way. Laugh. Give yourself permission to rest. **Look at what you can do.** Face the bumps with a smile. Life is full of surprises – be adaptable. Keep learning. Make achievable goals. Stay connected. Ask for help. Make lists. **Choose to be happy.** Work out to great music. Don't procrastinate. Make it happen. The best things in life are free. Don't be afraid to begin. Book friends time. Style points count – make the effort. Pick up the phone and call. Be young at heart. No regrets. Take different routes. Try new things. Challenge yourself. Book walk and talk time together. Positive energy is contagious. Be authentic. Commit. Hang out with positive people. Rise above adversity. Give back. Love the new you – bigger by experience. **Feel good moments – freeze frame. It's all about the come back, show them it's possible.** Believe in yourself when it's hard. Determination wins. **Switch on your second engine when it seems hard.**

It is the hardest times that bring out the deepest determination. More adversity in the family and my urgent gallbladder surgery, it felt that good days were ahead. Then more pain – another broken bone, a displaced wrist fracture in the same arm again. Reduced under anaesthetic and casted so awkwardly, I was again out of action on the tennis court and fatigue and pain ruled again. This time, others were less confident about my come back. This was not cancer. I knew if I had got through that year, I could get through this – I just had to convince everyone else not to give up on me. I was too broken for the practices on court, my wrist would no longer turn, and it was up to me to get back to the team. Dig deep and this is how positive card # 5 came along.

Balance

I rushed from work to the fracture clinic – nightmares of missing the cast removal and zing, off came the cast. I'm not sure what I was expecting – that I would shake it out and on I would go? It looked like it didn't belong to me. I looked at the huge swollen mound of wrist, stiff with withered muscles like an old lady. Oh it is so hard to manage balance. My enthusiasm meter flies off the scale nowadays and I want to try it all, like a kid in a candy store. Learn more, do more, explore more, change more, travel more, visit more, help more and appreciate more. Getting knocked down reminds me about balance yet I never want to lose that spirit.

Let's strive for balance but never to lose the brightness and spontaneity that defines us.

* * *

Balance

As I fell I just knew what I had done
Smashed up my wrist, just having fun
How can I learn the balance I need?
Life is a thrill on which I feed
Can I imagine and let my mind fill
With pulsing excitement of facing that hill
I try to relax and it helps balance me
Mindfully breathing – a moment to be
Calm with excitement; meter my mind
Measure my energy, quietness find
My mood is replenished when in that flow
Happiness, winning – where I love to go
Not for medals or titles, status or name
Win my own battles to help me reframe
So I have discovered I must blend the two
Relax my mind but let energy renew
Catharsis of sweat takes my mind to that place

Where energy rules and feelings embrace
Happiness takes over, troubles are less
Hit out those demons and worries confess
So balance is key, know there's always a way
Blending energy with calmness makes a good day

Grace

I was humbled by an unexpected discovery. I nervously went to a group, fragile to comparison, afraid to hear a story that I felt would derail me or compare inappropriately to mine. If you believe that people come into your life for a reason or you choose to notice them because it is the right moment, I noticed this person. It was not for what she had, but the grace of peace with which she handled it. It was such a discovery that her resolve, faith and inner peace was unforgettable – that is Grace.

* * *

Grace

A flow of movement I would say
But now I see it another way
Grace to suffer and not complain
Hit the bottom and rise again
Not to compare, radiate true
Not to pretend and be the real you
On your journey, facing fears
Feeling scared and shedding tears
Letting go of who you were
Discovering strength that we prefer
Grace to endure this difficult fight
Stepping forwards with all your might
No need for medals in this race
Fulfillment around us – that is grace

Fatigue

You may think I am talking about the sheer exhaustive pain of surgery or the poisonous chemo that knocked my socks off and left my brain so tired that it is beyond comparison. Another fatigue that people don't appreciate is the part that you don't see. It is easy to think that when the hair is growing back and the physical wounds heal that I am well again. Cancer is not like that. The thoughts are consuming, the demons of recurrence play their music loud at night and invade quiet times in the car. I drown them out with music, sing and tame them with my positive thinking phrases. Learning to live at peace with the emotional side of this disease takes work. My enthusiasm for the beauty of life and its wonderful people, quickly drained my batteries, especially initially back at work. Giving myself permission to do less was a lot harder than it seems.

There is resentment to cancer for taking this energy and there is difficulty putting myself up the priority list since it was felt that this was behind me. I had to learn to look at life differently because, after all, "Only the healthy me is helpful." It is easier to look at pills, supplements and food to control this but to understand that fatigue is related to our emotional damage seems so much harder.

* * *

Fatigue

For nights I wondered what the biopsy might show
So I practiced the worst scenario
Over and over, not sleeping a wink
Until the day that made my heart sink
An ordeal so hard that time was a blur
Nothing could prepare me for this to occur
Survival is instinct and panic so real
My mind racing forwards to plan this ordeal
First came the surgeries along with the pain
Nausea from drugs and fatigue hit again

Chemo had tiredness all of its own
And drugs that caused pain deep in the bone
It slowed down my mind so tired and unclear
Affecting my thinking gave me great fear
That my mind couldn't recall or calculate well
On the surface I functioned but inside I could tell
After the chemo more surgery came
No chance to get strong or get back to the same
Then back to work, small steps I would take
But talking and thinking left such a headache
The fatigue was consuming to keep up the pace
But the cogs started turning and soon I could face
The pulse of excitement without too much ill
Keeping cancer away with one little pill
Not to forget where I had been
And share with my patients what I had seen.

Quiet Time

Quiet Time Poem

I love to play tennis, talk and make friends
But quiet time too is where my mind mends
Up in my cabin painting the lake
Alone in the kitchen with time to bake
Silence is golden – I need it to heal
Time to think and time to feel
I love my work, it makes me thrive
But I live my life on overdrive
Take your mind to a place of peace
Where time stands still and thoughts release
The hardest part is permission for this
Life is consuming and these moments we'll miss.

* * *

I love to finish a 1000 piece puzzle. My son says old people do that. I always love doing challenging puzzles but I hope I get old too. It seems so huge when you start it but every time I passed by the table I put 10 more pieces together. First it takes permission to slow down, then to dismiss feelings that you are not doing anything constructive – but you are. My brain is looking to align the pieces as it comes together, calm in meditative thought eliminating intrusive thoughts and a focus that is so unwinding.

Find the time to have a coffee and a good book – make it a priority. This is not the one you have to read for book club but the one you always wanted to read when you had time. We all have our favourites. Find "That place in your head where time stands still."

Lessons on Quiet Time

Give yourself permission
Everybody needs some quiet space
It's all about getting started on a quiet project
Book the time to do it – walk, paint, read, do a puzzle, cook for fun
It should not be last on the list
Keep it on your "To Do" list – it is just as important
Be proud of what you accomplish and remember the process
Dare to do it
The hardest part is starting it.

Grounding

Grounding is a technique to redirect your train of thoughts as they sweep along that path of anxiety, imagining one thing after the next until life seems overwhelming. It may be triggered by a word, behaviour or some new results.

It is a method of staying in the present moment by healthy distraction, consciously noticing things around you and redirecting your thoughts to focus on your five senses, bringing things to the present. It is easy to do and practice and helps to calm the moment.

* * *

Grounding

When painful memories enter my head
I focus on now – a good place instead
I remember that feeling as I carve and lean
Hearing my snowboard and feel extreme
The lapping of waves hitting the shore
My cottage is quiet, the calm I need more
Remember the sound of a topspin shot
The sweat of a win, the sun so hot
Wine on the dock at the end of the day
Feet feel the rocks, friends chat and stay
Water at sunset glimmers all red
Serenity, beauty, peace in my head
Note things around you yellow or pink
Distract your mind; it will rethink
Connect new paths, old ones gone
Fears are grounded, moving on

Time

Time is assumed to always be there
A schedule so full there was nothing to spare
School and work, activities and more
There were people I didn't leave time for
Then came the news and time stood still
It all felt surreal – how could I be so ill
One step at a time, I lived day to day
Friends were there daily to help on my way
Neglected priority for friends I then found
And realized their importance so turned it around
Now balance is crucial in moving along
No excuses to visit before it's all gone
You only have one life so treasure those dear
Don't wait for cancer to make this all clear.

When Are You Better?

When are you better, will that day be
In 5 years or 10 years, or never be free
It's all about risk, how stats play their role
Or look at us harder, me as a whole
Is there a time when I'll worry no more
Will time heal that fear, who knows for sure
So we learn to live better, soak up each day
A lesson and realize no one can say
That we all have one life and how fragile it is
It can be taken as fast as it gives
Like ships in life we must sail and explore
Don't stay in harbour that's not what they're for.

Today

Why did it take cancer to help me see today?
Today was simply a path to tomorrow
Now it is smelling Christmas turkey
It is enjoying the pleasure of silence
It is holding hands deeply in the present
It is making it through a rough day of chemo
Knowing that I am fighting
It is the sweet hit in tennis
The feeling of speed on my snowboard
It is wakeboarding at warm sunset
To music that lifts your soul
Doing new things to be proud
While going a bit further than you want
Enjoying the present without fear
Today is manageable
As past evidence reinforces
I have the strength to get through
All adversity and stress
Living today.

The Lake

I can feel the smooth, cold water rushing past my ears as I dive in the lake. It feels confidently familiar yet dark, deep and unknown. I love the cleansing feeling as I rise to the surface. I feel in control in the water as I arch my body to the surface and the speed thrills me. This is my healing place.

It is this strange place that I exist at the moment, always worried of the unknown but some confidence that I will face what comes to me because I got this far. I have more inner strength than I could have ever realized.

The Lake

To realize the size of news
And what it meant that I could lose
As waves continued in spite of me
Tell me the path through adversity
The lake answered in its size
That from the depths I would rise
Like swimming strong in a storm
Perseverance and fortitude I would form
Freedom to drive my powerful boat
Time to swim, relax and float
Find some energy to fly in the air
Take off on the wakeboard while they stare
And I can forget that I wear a hat
As I fly through the air and realize that
Cancer can't get me when I'm in this space
A moment without it, time only can chase
And soon those good moments add to make more
A place in my head that I live life for
Never forget this, remember to share
Love all those moments and push yourself there.

Gardening

Gardening is often underestimated in its effectiveness. It is a physical activity, it is relaxing as your head unwinds and the wonder of a flower or bean emerges from a seed. It is being in the present and watching nature's little miracles, which are so rewarding. Remember to book gardening into your schedule. It is not only about the result, but what happens to you as you garden that we must notice. Notice your thoughts as you plant your annuals or bean seeds and how the silence affects you. Remember what it feels like to pick tomatoes and eat them. The best part is that we can look forward to doing it again next season.

* * *

Gardening Poem

That April when I sewed the seeds
My health took on its new needs
Drastic surgery made me weak
Through the window I could peak
Broken shoulder then shattered wrist
My stamina took on a whole new twist
More fallow garden years ahead
And treatments filled my time instead
But now I'm better, and spring arrives
A brand new vegetable garden thrives
Who would know that's what I need
Fresher greens on which to feed
The quiet and calmness, watching it grow
Stay with the process – that mindful flow.

Let's Talk About Stress

Do I get anxious about this cancer stuff still? Of course I do. Imagine as a doctor, every ache and pain is a self-diagnosis but I would drive myself crazy if I wasn't able to be sensible – when to go to a colleague for an opinion or when to realize that time is a good tool and problem solving a likely sprain is reasonable. So, when someone asks me a similar question, I get it, I have been there – it is worse at the beginning, expected. There is no crystal ball, the roulette wheel is uncertain – we just have to trust what we have. We have reassuring experts and I too am able to put myself in those shoes. It is a strange vulnerability as a doctor to admit humanness and fear as there is a self-expectation of perfection and in order to be strong for others, we cannot be allowed to be weak. I am exploring a new world of authenticity. It radiates truth and, in being clearly you, there is a risk of vulnerability but more importantly of reaching and connecting to the truth in others. To know where I have been physically is grounding. But to know that I am there on their emotional recovery too, takes a risk of revealing a side that many keep closed and behind the white coat.

As usual, this is the kind of entry that I least like to share since it makes me vulnerable to weakness and not my strength, which I am more comfortable talking about. However, if I can prove authenticity and show there is life beyond cancer and techniques to put your mind there, then I think I will make more of a difference. It is hard, it goes against the comfort zone of living behind the white coat but I want to show people that living as a doctor and patient can bring out the best in you and the risk of being authentically real is worth the price.

I get worried about being stressed since stress can lower our immunity, which is not ideal in cancer. There is a fine line to keep – good stress: bad stress. Good stress in exercise and a satisfyingly busy day releases good endorphins – serotonin and dopamine to make you feel good. I remember when I got cancer; the most distressing part was that I didn't know of anyone who hadn't closed his or her practice. Yes, my job takes a lot of energy and multi-tasking, but it was the saddest part to think that I may lose all I had worked for. Maybe that's what drove me to show you that it doesn't have to turn out that way, even when many bad layers happen. It was clear that my patients never gave up on me coming back, neither did my colleagues. That's what it takes. I love what I do, it creates fulfillment and I cannot imagine a life without it but it is not a smooth line, sometimes an amazing discovery of ourselves and we must be mindful to self check and manage bad stress, not escape from it but to know and reflect on the strength that we found through the hardest times of our lives in cancer treatment.

So Remember

Bravery is not measured by the thickness of your armour but the heart within.
Strength is not measured in muscle size but the tenacity to hold on.
The smartest minds are those who figure it out when it seems impossible, not the top score.
And friends never give up on you; so neither should you.

SECTION 6

Family

Positive Thinking Card 6

> ### Resilience
>
> **Resilience is post-traumatic growth. Life only makes sense backwards.** I will manage – just control what you can. Adapt. Do your best, people understand you are human. Coffee. Take a walk. **Rules weren't made to be personal.** Look at the big picture. I am an emotional survivor. **Break it down into pieces that are reachable.** Make a list – check it off. Print a calendar. Be prepared. Laugh. Bake and have fun with the adventure. Look around – I am blessed. Shop on line. Chat online. Lower expectations. Enjoy the day in minutes. Get an app for that. Watch expiry dates. Download a movie for hospital waits. **Hang out with positive people.** Don't cancel getting together with friends. Keep the tennis game. Email works. It will work out in the end – trust that. These are just bumps in the road. Own it. Work with it. Live. Plan a trip. Stay positive. Create. Paint. Share the excitement. Life is great – feel it. **Self check too**. Think of solutions not problems. Mothers say wise things. Keep thoughts constructive, not destructive. Say thank you every day.

The coach tracked me down on the far tennis court – "Your husband is on the phone, there's an emergency at the school". Has that ever happened to you? Your heart sinks but then it doesn't. My brain is thinking of a thousand medical scenarios – I can handle it.

After a recent run of broken bones myself, I realized the empowerment that all the recent adversity has given me. Not that this was cancer, but it was just one more thing on my list of recent challenges and I realized the resilience we have mastered.

On the same day my father was having more tests for his lung cancer and my world was a little more fractured with cancer impacting a close friend. I rushed to the school to find my son with a badly twisted broken leg. As we came into my hospital Emergency Room, familiar faces greeted me. We breathed through the pain, as they could not get the morphine in collapsing IVs. There was a remarkable understanding of suffering between us. It was going to need plates and screws to hold the splintered bones together.

I could manage: cancel this, cancel that, move office patients, mobilize friends to look after other necessary rides. It was a bump in my road. You adjust. Then as the dust settled, I wondered why I could cope, why so much more adaptive and accepting? Resilience.

Psychological Resilience is a dynamic process of positive behavioural adaptation to cope with significant stress and adversity associated with negative outcomes. It is known as **"Post-traumatic Growth,"** where the adverse experience leads to improved functioning and outlook. It is clearly a process of coping, rather than an individual's genetic trait or population characteristic. I might call it positive thinking.

The fascinating thing though, is that there are certain factors that predict increased resilience.

- The ability to **cope** with stress effectively and in a healthy manner
- Personal attributes including **outgoing, bright, positive self image**
- **Family** having close bonds and emotionally stable
- **Community** – support and counsel from peers
- Having good **problem-solving skills**
- Willingness to **seek help**
- Holding the belief that there is something one **can do** to manage your feelings and cope
- Having good **social support**
- Being connected with others – **family and friends**
- **Self-disclosure** of the adversity/trauma to loved ones
- **Spirituality**
- Having an identity as a **survivor** as opposed to a victim
- **Helping others**
- Finding **positive meaning** from the adversity/trauma

This is a skill that is learned – something that we can be trained to do if we allow ourselves to open up and be authentic. Little did I realize how much this would help for the future? What a paradox!

POSITIVE THINKING CARDS CREATE RESILIENCE!

So how can we build resilience? It is suggested the following are ways we can do this:

- Maintain **close relationships** with friends and family
- **Avoid** seeing crises or stressful events as **unbearable**
- **Accept** circumstances that are **out of your control**
- Develop **realistic goals** and move towards them
- Take **decisive actions** in adverse situations
- Look for opportunities of **self-discovery** after struggle with traumatic loss
- Develop **self-confidence**
- Keep perspective and consider the **broader context**
- **Visualize healing,** expecting good things
- Take care of mind and body by **exercising** regularly, **noticing** one's own **needs and feelings**

So when your mountain seems all uphill, realize the gruelling training you are undergoing and that looking at every day in a positive outlook will serve you well for your future and those around you.

Every Fighter Pilot Needs A Good Wingman

I was reminded of how much stronger we are when that wingman flies in formation with us to fight the cancer enemy.

A wingman is a pilot who supports another in a potentially dangerous flying environment. Wingman was originally a term referring to the plane flying beside and slightly behind the lead plane in an aircraft formation.

The traditional military definition of a "Wingman" refers to the pattern in which fighter jets fly. There is always a lead aircraft and another that flies off the right wing of and behind the lead. This second pilot is called the "Wingman" because he or she primarily protects the lead by "watching his back."

The wingman's role in combat is to add the element of mutual support to aerial combat. The wingman makes the flight both offensively and defensively more capable by increasing firepower, situational awareness, attacking an enemy threatening a comrade, and most importantly the ability to employ more dynamic tactability.

The amazing thing is that before cancer I did not know the amazing power and dedication of these people. Off that wing I could always count on a few amazing people – steadfast with the endurance to fly the whole journey and beyond. In fact, working together through the storm of cancer, our strength together, far exceeds our individual power when that second pilot flies next to you to protect you. Yes, it's your journey alone to fight but don't forget the power of a good wingman. Fly in formation and look for him over your right shoulder at all times – he is there.

How Do You Tell Kids About Cancer?

(Diary entry April 2010)
I was numb. It was surreal, like I was hearing the news about someone else. I was shaking. I hate reading that word "invasive". I keep getting waves of panic with sweats over me.
I have to tell the kids in 20 minutes. This is sickening.

Do you tell them? How much do you tell them? How will they react? Will they think I will die? Will they cope?

There are many different situations with cancer that unfold but I want to reflect on several life experiences including my own for those who echo that horrible issue of talking to your kids – to be honest while dealing with the maternal feeling to protect them from your deepest fears and convey strength, hope and togetherness as a team.

Yes, my kids were young teens. Life revolved around their schedule and self-image played a big role at that age. Being singled out with a bald cancer mum was not on their agenda and I was asked by my son to always wear a wig or not to show up at school initially. It hurt more than the cancer. It hurt them too. They were not in denial – to control their world and keep order was controlling the chaos too. I always say time is a great tool and in this case, of course, the treatment was too long not to embrace the changes; then the big issue that the BRCA genetic mutation discovery could affect them.

Somewhere in the course of surgeries and weakness, the attitude changed again – resentment to my special status as they took on more chores and still, only I got the gifts and cards. I learned from this as my daughter broke down and taught me this understanding – that people don't notice how hurt the kids are. In fact, they were packed off to activities in generous friends' cars or school rides without much choice.

So why burden them with cancer details?

Because, they got it – they knew what cancer was. They needed to hear it was treatable. They needed to know that there was nothing we did to cause this. I couldn't carry all the burden of treatment and they would learn that they could manage more with our support. Life isn't fair and you should not have to learn this at their age but by being open about this is a promise of truth and to give them the skills to get through adversity.

We forget that kids are smart and resilient and furthermore, they can be our strength and deliver refreshing optimism. They are the ones who burst through the doors with artwork and energy that brings a smile to your worn out body. They make you laugh at the small things and never let anything get in the way of vacation planning – of course you will be there. They proudly run to support the hospital because of their mum. They walk in relay for life with you and my daughter arranged for me to do a speech and to hold the banner with my father who battled cancer too as we walked the first lap together. Words of strength on her lantern sting as I see it on the relay route. She has risen to challenges so much bigger now with courage, confidence and independence. She is in biomedical science, determined to study medicine, sure of the progress of science and cancer treatment.

It was tough on them; guilt we have to come to terms with. I included them because we had to face it as a team – strength and truth together was essential. Now cancer is an accepted part of our vocabulary and we celebrate the milestones and reflect of the journey. Their genetic BRCA testing will be done when they are ready to handle the choices of a positive result. It will not go away – we will be united together.

Family Poem

What's it like on the other side?
To watch and hurt through cancer's ride
The journey's so tough on my family too
The guilt that it brings lands right back on you
Fear is huge and helpless they feel
A disease and words that still seem unreal
Kids try to keep all things the same
But hurt to see that it's to blame
To work and cook and manage the drives
Not a word of complaint, it changes our lives
To protect is instinct but doesn't work here
Giving comfort, reassurance and a listening ear
But from the bad comes the good as we all play our role
The burden of cancer did not take its toll
It strengthened our spirit and made us all one
We spend time together and focus on fun
As a family we found closeness in the troubles we face
And treasure moments together we'll never replace.

How Cancer Changes Us – A Teen's Perspective:

I included this, to never underestimate a child's mind. To protect them is instinct but sharing your journey can give them spirit and wings of resilience that can inspire you.

My teenage daughter was booked to go on an educational exploration of Central America, including some volunteer projects just months after my diagnosis. I encouraged her to go, not to feel worried or held back by my cancer and to grow as a person on this trip. She was learning with teachers and volunteering in a Guatemalan Hospital and Health Center as well as organic planting projects. There was structure and safety but no luxury for the teenagers. They were required to write educational diaries. She shared a powerful journal entry with me and said that her teacher had cried as she had expressed the heartfelt answer to the day's question. We always wonder how our kids handle it. We want to protect them but we can only help them handle it. With her permission, here is a personal glimpse. It takes a lot to share these feelings publically, I am so respectful of her willingness to allow us in – we rarely see inside their minds.

* * *

What event has shaped your life?

An event that has shaped my life was my mom getting diagnosed with breast cancer. I have always been really close with her and it was one casual school night, after some days preceding an amazing family trip, that I heard the life changing news. At first I cried. I cried for the thought of losing her and never receiving her bottomless love and guidance ever again. It was in the weeks following though, that I noticed a change in her attitude and mine. I started appreciating every talk and every moment I spent with her. She had to stay home from work of course, because of all the surgery and chemotherapy, but this meant for the first time, she had been home when I came home from school. She had more time to just talk to me and help me with anything I needed. When she was working, we did not have time for this. From her hardships and our talks, it brought out the best in me. I was inspired to study harder, to play harder for my school teams and just find positive in every situation I faced.

My marks and hard work paid off. I have never been so determined to accomplish something before. Having a mother with a life-threatening disease and the threat of losing her brought out the determination in me. I also really think it was her remarkable and inspiring positive attitude through the long journey to better health that caused my sudden urge for accomplishment. She shaped my life and as I think about her; I forget about her illness because it is her positive energy that touched everyone around her and caused him or her to live to the fullest that was so remarkable. Life is a precious thing and it is not until it is threatened do we thank ourselves for what we have lived and understand its price. From complaining about going to tennis practice or fussing with my hair, I now can easily remind myself of the things my mom can do, do not include those. I quickly thank "Him" for what he has given me and clear out the negative atmosphere from the room. I am a spiritual but not very religious person and I do thank all the stars above that I still have my mom, my family and follow my positive view on life.

* * *

If you were to change anything about yourself, what would it be?

I was not a very determined person before my mom's cancer diagnosis. From all this experience, I have developed a stronger initiative to fulfill more of my life goals and to appreciate every experience I go through. Finding a positive attitude in a difficult situation is a skill and I believe I have developed this skill further, being inspired by my mom's amazing outlook on life. I hope to fulfill all my goals, reflecting some of the positive energy my mom has been showing me. I had been more scared to face difficult things in life before this. With a new courageous and ambitious attitude, I am realizing how much more there is to enjoy in life. This is what I am attempting to change about myself – to make myself a better person benefits me, and all those around me.

Finding ambition within yourself to live your life fully becomes addicting and keeps you striving for higher goals. This is what I want to change about myself: to become a person, like my mother, who spends every waking minute to find the most positive things in life and spend her time doing the things she loves most. Having an attitude like this makes my cottage more beautiful, my dog more loving, my teachers more exciting and my life more successful. I hope in the future that one day I can look back at my mom, free of cancer, and see a girl that changed her life by finding attitude and strength from her mom to live her life to the fullest and achieve her big dreams.

My daughter
Age 16

Nano – My Dog

Licking my tears his eyes would say
Tell me your problems, I'll take them away
Those big brown eyes all watery and deep
The warmth of his body against me sleep
Connected to me like invisible string
He protected me from everything
He was my coach to make me walk
A listening ear for me to talk
Even on worst days of sickness and pains
We'd walk a block with dangling drains
Opening the door I hear the scurry
Of happy feet to greet in a hurry
Licks of gratitude because I am there
That pure simple love is what they share.

SECTION 7

Friends

Positive Thinking Card 7

> ### Remember What I Have Got
>
> **LOVE** – someone who shows his love, not just says it – my rock. **SUPPORT** – they understand and protect me- my colleagues, my friends. **DETERMINATION** – showing I can do it, no excuses. **FITNESS** – look how far I have come – looking good, feeling great, overcome obstacles. **POSITIVE ATTITUDE** – there's always a way, adapt. **INTELLIGENCE** – learn new things, get it back, think fast, try hard. **FRIENDS** – they all appeared when I needed them most. **MY JOB** – my vocation, to make a difference, how it felt to loose that then get it back. **SINCERITY** – authenticity is the only way to be. **EMPATHY** – it stings because you've been there but your path is your own. **STRENGTH** – of mind and body never tested so much. **CREATIVITY** – the silent therapy within my brain. **EXPERIENCE** – to be on both sides and pass on the coping tools, to understand. **PERMISSION** – to rest, to play, to be enough. **FAMILY** – always there, always a shoulder to lean on. **SPIRIT** – contagious, adventurous, fit it all in, smile. **PURPOSE** – believe in yourself and your path.

I had to train myself hard to think differently – not to take your head down the scary path of nothing is going right but to believe that every hurdle stands a chance of a good outcome despite past events and that I must believe that. It is normal that our heads go down the cancer path of bad outcomes but if we can notice that thought and change its direction – exchange it for a positive or constructive thought, it makes so much difference.

While painting this weekend, I had to look at the picture and think differently. Instead of painting a tree that was in the picture, I had to notice everything around the picture and paint the negative space to make the tree seem like it was outlined. A parallel to my approach to life – to look at what I have, not focus on the obvious piece but what is around it – notice the unnoticeable…take the negative and make it your positive and you will stand out of the crowd…

Feeling exhaustion at the end of my day
Because I had the chance to make a difference

The extra 10 minutes at my desk
Because that person needed a phone call and it felt good

Not worrying about an imperfect house of chores
Because it means I have a home

Contemplating those times in a traffic jam
Because I have the privilege of a car

Taking the furthest parking space
Because I can walk

Tolerating aches in the morning
Because getting older is a privilege not an expectation

Accepting little things that may previously upset you
Because people would move heaven and earth to help me

Not needing my hair to look perfect
Because now I have hair again, period

Not focusing on what I can't change
Because changing what you can makes it all work better

Friends

When cancer hits a deadly blow
And fighting so hard is where you must go,
Colleagues come from far and wide
To offer help and be by my side
Surgeon, doctor, nurse or friend
Skill of the knife or listening ear lend
Giving their talents is all they can do
Making the journey is all up to you
The sickness and pain is so hard to bear
But around every corner my friends are all there
To cheer me on like the crowd of a race
And pull me on to keep up the pace
Every stride, every minute moves to the past
Through chemo and surgery and on to the last
But last is a hard one, as all of you know
A living uncertainty time only will show
When asked what I learned most of all I can tell
Was friendship of colleagues to help me get well
You never can see till it's taken away
How much of you loves to help people each day
Returning to hugs a patient tells me
That we all have a path and how big mine will be.

Dear Friend

The fragile voice of a friend catapulted me back to last April when my world stood still. I could feel her reeling with fear and trying to be brave. My heart broke for her and I wanted to be there to just hold her up like so many people held me up as my strong legs buckled. Our journeys are all different and only you can discover them but the strength of many, as you put on your war paint for battle, lifts and supports your spirit. It is this courage that we all have within us that helps us step forward. Saying farewell to the old you to trust your raw, hurt self, takes courage when the bearing ahead is so uncertain. So living in the present is the best recipe. Striving for wellness and accepting ourselves is all we can do because "all we can do is always enough."

We must celebrate our warrior circle where the power of many helps these people climb huge mountains and lets them know they are not alone. That step at a time seems like a ladder so steep, unable to see the top – but you will know when you are there. The mist will eventually lift and you will know where you have been and why.

* * *

Dear Friend

A fragile voice, I can't believe what I heard
The size of the news is beyond any word
My heart felt your pain and terrible fear
I'll be here to question, to make it more clear
One day at a time is all you can do
Trusting your doctors helps to heal you
I am here cheering every step of the way
Moving forward is progress every day
Live in the present and do all those things
Like drawing with kids and playing on swings
Ask for some help that's what we are for
And friends and your family will be at your door

You'll realize how special you really are
As friends come to hold you from near and far
You have more strength than you'll ever know
The power of spirit is now what you show
I know that you'll get there; you'll show the world how
So stay close together and live in the now
And put on your war paint, to battle you go
With strength and courage, you are our hero

3 Friends

For my breast cancer "sisters."

Friends reunited through the same cause
That breast cancer hit us to make our lives pause
We grew up as neighbours loosing touch as you do
But have now shared our journey, helped each other get through
In pain we related, have a lunch, lend an ear
Not to compare but help with the fear
We all have a story, each step is your own
But embracing those sisters helped you feel less alone
We radiate energy as awakened we feel
To know we faced danger and now life is real
So we wake up so grateful, you never would know
How precious your friends are, what support they can show
And stay in the present, except I can see
When we reflect on this journey as friends over tea.

SECTION 8

Difficult Things

Positive Thinking Card 8

Own it

Go beyond your comfort zone, you'll be proud of yourself. Be amazed. Be inspired. Be humbled. Don't let time run out, fit it all in. Prove that you can do it. Take educated risks. No regrets or maybe's. Be prepared but do it. Be proud of myself. Learn new things. You can do it, make it happen. Think of a way. Flip your thinking. Determination is a forward direction. Challenge yourself but don't stress yourself. **Be the change. Own it – share it- inspire with it.** Goalify. **Notice your thinking**. Priorities. Push yourself. Finish. Examine guilty feelings and correct them. Be kind to yourself too. Remember to laugh. **Doors open – see them – walk through them**. Learn new things. Own your disease. Share the wisdom. Inspire with your change. Don't overthink. Let it go.

Control – Learning Not To Have It All

Control – my biggest problem in dealing with cancer. Like an avalanche, it knocked me sideways and just as I tried to gain control; I lost it again and again. That horrible feeling as you desperately try to find the path through all the results. It was topped off by the BRCA mutation discovery that knocked me sideways again, lead carefully out of the counselling room to be offered a therapist when it hadn't even sunk in what this all meant. And so, control was seriously rocketing downwards, like a car with no brakes. Could I work again? Did people believe I could get through this? Actually, who would believe, that, like India, I would come back changed and inspire so many – the outcome and control of the future being so much less relevant that what I bring and how I now think.

"Sign here" he said, "it's a four year cellphone plan with a penalty to break it," the assistant kindly told me. I don't think past the next season and that's a great improvement. A part of me makes exciting plans for the next adventure but four years – that's a gamble I can't do. And then my car, another one, I am fully responsible for my 4 year ownership – no problem, I'm strong now says the good side of my head. After all, as I always say, no one knows what is around the corner, but four years, that's the oncology clinic talk.

Is it just me or, does everybody who has had cancer have this fleeting fight with their awareness? I know that there is a good probability that I will do well with all my treatment but a little tiny dark part of my mind knows that cancer is not like having your appendix out – it has a risk and that is what haunts us.

It is easy to see why people do not tell clients or work colleagues; for fear of thinking their commitment is risky. What a precipice we sit on. We have to acknowledge the thoughts yet not allow them to define us.

As you know, I don't live life on the edge, except going to India! – I am the most conservative, safety conscious person around. Yes, most people could not believe I signed up, including me. It was something inside me that wanted to push myself outside my comfort zone. I wanted to prove that I could go further before time ran out, not live life with regrets or maybe's, be proud of myself, open to learn new things, be humbled, be amazed, be inspired and take risks. In fact, this year, I have rapidly been checking the bucket list – "meet a old friend." On my way to India, I met with my school friend of twenty-five years ago and madly rushed around London seeing people who had not seen me since cancer. Scared stiff, I managed to check off parasailing, zip lined the canopy with my family recently and rode a camel from the Taj Mahal viewpoint right back to my bus – not getting on by ladder – no, the camel stood up like a giraffe sending me clinging for my life to the rickety chair.

The difficult side of going to India is certainly the lack of hygiene, the disease and infestation, the dirt and poverty that is such a contrast to the beautiful people.

I always said that I write best when emotions are hurting. As I relive the decisions, I want to hold those thoughts, the ones that helped me decide. There will be times in my life when something else comes along, another door opens, and I will decide to open it because experience now tells me it is worth trying. And so I hold another thinking card – one that contains all those forward thinking words, ready for next time…

I learned on the plane, on my way to India, a very valuable lesson from the wise man who sat next to me, interested in the documentary I was watching: He told me, *"A challenge is when you have to try and do something and you have the tools. But stress is when you have to do something and you don't have the tools – it's different: Say yes and challenge yourself, but be careful to see that you don't stress yourself."*

Think Before You Talk, But Please Talk

Those Crazy Cancer Comments

That takes me back to those early days in cancer diagnosis with the funniest comments. As a doctor, I certainly knew about cancer but I had a lot to learn about what it felt to have your life on the line and everything you ever worked for and held precious, taken away, turned upside down with uncertainty meeting you at so many corners. Decision-making was something I had trained for years to do. Trained in Special Competency in Emergency Medicine, I could make adrenaline-pumped decisions – but I had never faced the worst decisions – my own health with a loss of control that felt like dreaded free-fall sometimes.

So, people felt they should advise me:

Everyone seemed to know someone "who had what I had" – unfortunately, I know too much – I knew the surgery they had or the age or lack of chemo meant it was not the same. I could not say anything but be angry inside. Frustrated that they could not see it, trying to acknowledge that they wanted to help. "I can give you their number," they would add. I could not talk to someone who didn't understand the level of understanding I had at that point. I trusted my colleagues who also became my resources. I could talk with them.

"I have a gift for you – some resource pamphlets" – I **%$ know the resources – I am a doctor – just hug me! I am a real person too. It was those people who saw me as the real, authentic, hurt human being that were special. Many were also scared at the beginning. The words were a response that avoided getting too close.

"So many more people have cancer nowadays," is another statement I never perfected my answer towards. It did not make me feel better in the least. On uncovering a painful family history of young ovarian cancer and dealing with my new BRCA mutation, I had trouble agreeing with their statement. I simply felt fortunate that I had the privilege of treatment and so much more hope than my earlier relatives.

"How are you eating differently since cancer?" many would ask. No, my food did not cause my cancer. I crave control like all of us and cancer gives us so little control. It comes upon us as an unfortunate aberrancy in cell division, which we have yet to understand completely. We know carcinogens like smoking are more likely to make this happen but let's not try extrapolating that to the microwave or TV screen. I was told that I was lucky to get this far with such a BRCA mutation so healthy eating and exercise I continue, address stress and live in the acceptance that life has randomness that we will never be able to control.

"I take naturopathic supplements to prevent cancer," aggravated my internal emotional confrontation. How do I handle these people? Everyone has a right to his or her own decisions but please don't think you are protected from cancer. It took every cell in my body to approach this in a professional manner to enable the person to see both sides and see the scientific evidence of health prevention in addition to their chosen additives. Remarkably, helping these people see the benefit of medical prevention and harmonize an approach can be incredibly rewarding. I have calmed too to be less hurt inside as my own wounds are less fresh. I simply let it go now.

"You will have to learn some crafts for your spare time," was a comment as I started my disability soon after my diagnosis. As I struggled to put together layers of bad news, I had to be constantly reminded that it was now time for me to be the patient, not to feel guilty and to understand that someone else could do my job for a while and it could be handled without me. This had the flip reaction of loosing a very fulfilling part of my life and learning to love a person without that. It has meant that I remind colleagues daily of the privilege of being a doctor, getting my career back felt like the day I got into medical school – never will I forget or take that for granted.

"My kids can tutor your kids with schoolwork." What did they miss? The reason my kids are not coping in school is because of me. Exams may need to be deferred and concentration is poor. The stress of cancer and the uncertainty it brings needs a hug and understanding, not tutoring. They need a trip out to the movies or a sleepover if you want to help. Don't forget them, they are hurt too – it's not just me going through cancer.

Maybe some of these hit a chord. Seriously though, they hurt at the time. Now I am able to laugh at the reactions I had. We are all unique in our journeys. Fortunately, after the rain, comes the best sunsets. I am not always talking about ideal outcomes but that magic you feel as you see all the good things around you and awaken with adversity. I can understand how people react when terrible news hits and how a listening ear and empathy can help. Being a real human being and authentic self as well as a doctor is the beautiful sunset that came out of my terrible rainstorm and I understand it so much more.

* * *

Think Before You Talk, But Please Talk

"Some people say the wrong things – don't be angry"

How did they tell you, was it sincere
Did they comfort your tears, give a listening ear
Did you freeze in your seat; who did you call
Was this nightmare real or will you wake from it all
What was your vision as tests reveal more
Like drowning in seas, trying to reach shore
"How are you now," they'd ask me, not wait for reply
I've just got cancer and afraid I might die
That's not what they heard; they are now far away
To them you passed by on an ordinary day
My aunt had what you have, my friend had it too
They now juice their diet, what are you going to do
I don't want the stats, or who you know died
How breasts aren't important or how long you cried
Just be the person who knows I'm still me
Come for a visit and a cup of tea
Sit and listen, cheer me on when weak
It's a long scary journey that can feel so bleak
Don't tell me I'm strong, sometimes I'm not
Don't tell me you know the pain that I've got

"I'll be fine" is telling you more than me
So I recite to myself the good things I see
I live in the present and love every day
There's not always next time so "yes" I now say
Your voice is important so email or phone
Just be yourself and I won't be alone.

Say The Word "Mastectomies"

I was talking to a nurse as I did my rounds at the hospital. "Wow, how are you doing?" she asked. "It's good to see you here working and so well" (I cant imagine anything else). "What was it like?" As I put the year into a nutshell, she was surprised at my openness: "You have to say mastectomies, it is real and you can look great," I emphasized. It broke down barriers and she revealed her history.

I remember the first time I said it when the second cancer was found in the other breast: "Is it related to the other cancer?" I asked the surgeon, still shaking from the news a few days earlier of the first egg-shaped cancer lump on the left side. "Just bad breast tissue" said the surgeon "What about…" I hesitated, "Yes, you can say it" he replied. "Mastectomies," I said. There was silent agreement. The plastic surgeon made it real and positive. We laughed as we selected the solid gel composite implants that looked convincingly real. We discussed size, perkiness and suddenly the loss of these horribly diseased breasts was being balanced by the confidence and security of her experienced wisdom and trust. Learning to live with that cancer shadow is reminded in the mirror. It is time to get to know the new you and that includes mastectomies. I remember in medical school 24 years ago, they made us say the word "sex" all the time – get used to saying it, it is a normal word and a regular part of our medical vocabulary. So is mastectomy. Now when people hesitate to ask me, I tell them – it is how I survived cancer and now part of me. Learn to let cancer and your mastectomies are part of your vocabulary and move forwards to let the world know that these words are part of you but not your identity. Say the word mastectomies; say the word cancer like we say the word sex.

Love Our Flaws – They Make Us Unique.

It has been said that we are like Opals – not clear diamonds but the amazing beauty of an opal lies in the desert dust, sand and silica within – owing its beauty, not to perfection but to the defects. The opal is full of minute fissures that allow air inside to refract the light in a rainbow of colours. There is no beauty of an opal in the dark; its lustre is only seen as it sits on the skin and soaks up the light that shines on its heart.

And so, we cannot dwell on the physical and emotional scars that we encounter but to realize that together they form brilliance in their unity. Not every problem works out perfectly but it is harmonizing these imperfections that create our sparkle and energy of character.

Like us, it is the flaws in an opal that allow the stone to become individual, valuable and unique.

Hair – Day 16

As I reflect on this time last year, I am reminded as I see other people reach day 16 – a reminder that this horrid nightmare is real and the effects of chemo take place. That's when you need hugs and hands to hold, reminding you of the strength of others around you to keep you going and hold you up – how looking good makes you feel better, helping to put on a smile when you are raw and wounded inside. So hold on to someone and find courage in the tough times and smile with my poem.

I hated it curly or even too long
But most of all I hated it gone
Facing the fact of wearing pretend
I asked for their votes on Facebook to send
Long or short, blond or brunette
Chestnut and straight with highlights I'd get
I joked with my husband not to get bald
But never to dream that mine could have falled
I loved my new wig so quick to get ready
Drawing my eyebrows I'd hold pencil steady
A scarf worked for tennis, getting fit was the key
A drawer of selection – stay matchy matchy
In shaving my head, for courage I prayed
Inspiring others to not be afraid
As I looked at my head, the good I could tell
Was the drug must be working to help make me well
So I put on my make up to help me look nice
To rid me of cancer, it's well worth the price

Everyone Has A Story

I remember times when I have prejudged someone – they are late or forgot an appointment. I thought I could judge the attitude before I knew the story. Now, I know as people look at me – they have no idea what I have been through but how humbling it can be as I find out their own tragedies. I see the pain of a mother loosing a child, or a spouse loosing their life long partner, growing up in war-torn situations and hurt for their story. So, as unusual as my crazy cancer story is, I remind myself every day that Everyone Has a Story.

When I had the waves of cancer diagnoses sequentially knocking my feet from under me I felt that I was the only one in this situation and so fragile to comparison. The fragility made me so weak however that help was my only way out. Slowly trusting to confide and getting very wise healing advice with my minister, I stepped into sharing extremely carefully. This lead to Wellspring and slowly going beyond my comfort zone realizing that I could listen to others and hear their stories without anger to comparison. Now, I enjoy sharing with others who have weathered adversity – to see their strength and grace. Some are dealing with bigger things, which are humbling – yes, we each have a journey – unique and special but fear unites us and can be an amazing bond.

Everyone has a story

Judging the outside is only to learn
To be wiser and humble on the next turn
Cancer is grounding to revalue life
Helps us to balance trouble and strife
But always to see it's not only us
Is it the person on the same bus?
Do they grieve loss in spouse or a child
Deep-rooted pain inside them filed
Look in the store to left and to right
Who else has handled a life of a fight
Maybe the person who lets me in line
Or a smile from a table as we all dine
We all have a story, treat them all well,
Don't judge the cover, you never can tell.

When You Can't Change The Outcome, You Can Change The Journey

Sometimes cancer is bigger than all the medicine and power we have. Things don't happen for a reason, cancer is cruel. We will never understand that part. So when the outcome is clear, we must focus on making the journey easier. This is the time that we do have left. It is the time to talk and reflect, love and hold. It is so important that it is not a lonely journey but to know that this next step is together and supported – as life begins, so there is end. Our spirit lives on. We need to know we matter, that our existence made a difference spiritually. Love hurts but it is never forgotten and leaves us changed. The risk of breaking our heart does not stop us giving our deepest love. So I leave you with these poems for those hardest times to go to that person's bedside and share words so that they are not alone.

* * *

When You Can't Change the Outcome,
You Can Change The Journey

A spirited person, why must it be you
Those words of more cancer cannot be true
But I realize and see the goodness around
The warmth of family and love that surround
You may not see all the hearts that you touch
To ground us and see what matters so much
It's those who are there when life is too hard
Do chores, bring the dinner or send a good card
The outcome is there but the journey not clear
More love and hearts help lessen the fear
We're always there night and day
To give you courage and light your way
Holding hands together when the times are tough
To know we are there can be just enough
Though the outcome is there, let's smile at today
And cherish the present that can't go away.

Its Not What's Important, It's Who's Important

In this season we rush to the store
Important gifts and who to buy for
Really however, it's all just stuff
If we look around we all have enough
The priceless gifts money can't buy
Are friends and family on whom we rely
They are there to hold your hand
And pick you up and help you stand
Recall good moments, there at your side
When things are rough, in them confide
Money can't buy them; they're grown from the heart
The truest of bond that love cannot part
They will be there night and day
Ease your fears to find your way
Cheer you up make you smile
Give a hug and stay a while
Your spirit brings them when the road is tough
Remember, it's who's important, not the stuff.

Sometimes there are no words to express bad news when someone close to you is dying of cancer – all you have is love, so many people thinking of that person – endless, bottomless love in their fight. I made this layered watercolour so that they could look at it on the wall knowing they are never alone on the journey, even when it is beyond my comprehension, I can offer love, knowing we are there.

Dream

Close you eyes and what do you see
Are you flying with wings feeling so free
Pain is no more, wind in your hair
Loved by your friends knowing they care
Cheering you on, your journey so tough
All you can do is always enough
Take time to rest, take time to dream
Of days in the summer and docks with ice cream
Angels on earth and those in the sky
To protect you as every day passes by
Close your eyes, we are never too far away
You're never alone through night and day
Bringing our energy, we can't be your fight
But can cheer you on to stay in the light
You make it all different, more than you know
Inspiring with courage is now what you show
Now take time to dream, take time to sleep
Protect you and love you, angels will keep.

Dream

– a watercolour and paper multi-media collage with salt sprinkled to give a snow effect.

Cherish Each Moment

For Ryan xo
When your fight seems too big and painful, break it down to moments.
That's what we do have.

*　*　*

Cherish Each Moment

A moment is a piece of time that you can feel right now
Focus on the present and you will see just how
A moment can be laughter; belly aching sore
A moment is a hug, as family leave the door
A moment is a lifetime whenever you are scared
A moment is a visit to tell a friend you cared
A moment is a heartfelt talk in the middle of the night
A moment is the time to send a card to help the fight
A moment is the feeling of flying through the air
A moment is the memory of going higher than you dare
In moments when you're hurting or facing hugest fears
Our hearts are there a thousand strong to help you with the tears
Have you ever missed the moment because your head was turned
You will not repeat that time again is all that you had learned
It's moments of embarrassment that we remember well
Let's laugh and think of growing up and stories we could tell
Your inspiration grounds us and we all can learn from you
To cherish every moment is what we all must do.

SECTION 9

Love

Positive Thinking Card 9

**Positive Thinking Card 9
Forgive Yourself**

Forgive yourself – you are not the first one to make that mistake. Put things in perspective. Change things. Plan ahead – just not too far. Have a plan B. Write down the day. Put it in the calendar immediately. Copy to everyone. Time has more minutes than you think. **Remember the good stuff.** Be sincere. Learn new things when old ones don't work. Rest your mind. Deal with the inbox – into the outbox. **Be the change you talk about. Give people a chance to try.** Prepare the night before. Grow vegetables. Learn about tea. Sew and create. Scrabble. Old movies together. Paddleboard. Blaze new trails. Influence others. It is what it is – some things can't change. Attitude is controllable. **Tomorrow is a brand new day.** A journey together feels so much better. Make a new wish every day. You can find light in the darkest places. Run, sweat, peace. Count good things. Run, sweat, feel better. Being alone sometimes feels good, sometimes not good – be OK with that. Permission to have a nap. Talking books. Love that person who holds your hand at every finish line! **Sometimes, saying yes makes extraordinary memories** – that's worth it. Figure it out. Delegate. **Remarkable people do not just happen.**

Love Poem

Beyond the scars my heart will glow
And feels the love that family show
Where would I be without you there
To hold my hand and know you care
This year has given us all a chance
To realize who's special, to hug, to dance
To live in the moment and love every day
A passion for life that won't go away
And teach each other to rise above
And climb great mountains because of LOVE

Forever

With the first words of cancer, in your heart there's a hole
The burden it gives goes deep to the soul
It takes your career, role as mother and wife
But you notice good things that start happening in life
Cancer doesn't scare him away
It makes us live each precious day
To love you inside, despite the drugs
And hold you tight and give you hugs
He sees the scars and baldness too
And says the smile is what makes you
How good it is to share the path
As chemo deals is sickening wrath
To remind us what we can be without
And to never look at the clouds of doubt
Despite a rash or painful sores
We focus on what's behind new doors
Genetics can be a frightening find
Accepting danger is hard for the mind
A soul mate for life despite all ills
Can help each other climb great hills
And from each other we learn great things
To love each day for what life brings
We'll toast some wine on trips far and wide
And deep snow at Whistler together we'll ride
We look to the positive to keep us strong
And enjoy being together our whole life long

I love

I was given a bag as a gift. On the front and the label were the instructions to write, "I love," fill in the blank. I thought I knew what to write but then realized there were so many things that I loved. I didn't realize until I thought about it. They are simple pleasures of everyday life that make it so special, and discoveries that adversity has opened my eyes to see. I can choose what to focus on in my head: those little demons that play back last year's terrifying movie of never-ending hurdles that still throw me curve balls or look at all the gifts that life brings me every day. I love these things. Just stop for a minute and fill in the blank too. I bet you can't stop at one thing.

* * *

I Love_____
I love Mark
I love my cottage
I love life
I love tennis
I love my family
I love my sister and how close we are now
I love the deep sincerity in my friends
I love wine at sunset on the lake
I love reading at 4pm on Saturday on the dock
I love sleeping in
I love the smell of fresh coffee on the weekend
I love lying down after a long day's work
I love baking on a rainy day
I love my art studio
I love deep powder snow
I love pulling up out of the water on my slalom ski
I love nailing a great wakeboard jump
I love dressing up to go out
I love surprises

I love giving
I love Christmas
I love diving in on a hot day
I love the sound of thunder when you are safe
I love making a difference in people
I love good red wine
I love dancing to great music
I love quiet time
I love Nano, my dog
Write your own "I love..." list

SECTION 10

Survivorship

Positive Thinking Card 10

> **Positive Thinking Card 10**
> **Remember The Process**
>
> **Remember the process, not just the result.** Put a value on that. Daily gratitude. Daily intentions. Meditation in movement. **Don't forecast.** Look at stumbling blocks differently. Forgive even the hardest things. **If it's not good for you, let go of that thought.** You are genuine – the right people see you for that. Don't prejudge. Go with the flow. Self check thinking. Filter words. Making change is not instant. **Be in the present.** Remember to celebrate everything. Try. How can you learn if you don't fail at something? Wisdom comes from learning from things that went wrong. Listen to wise people and learn from their mistakes. Trust your instincts. **Believe in purpose.** Believe your inner strength. **Believe that worlds collide when they are supposed to and stars align.** Believe that you can make a difference – that you matter. A soul to dare.

Survivorship is a process. Granted, surviving the wrath of chemo needs a celebration and getting through a year of so many scary surgeries is worth a bit of yahoo, but after that we are still surviving cancer. Cancer has treatment side effects from surgery, radiation and ongoing medication, emotional baggage from the fear of recurrence and the effort to pick up the pieces of everyday life as a mother and career is exhausting. Cancer takes away the innocence that we have our whole life in front of us and we must learn to live in the peace of its threat. Control is one of those successful traits that has paved paths of career success – cancer suddenly disrupts that control in such a savage way that our fragile soul is searching for security that will only be found in our healed self. Survivorship is a process we face everyday and we can choose to become empowered by our past.

What Is Survivorship?

Survivorship – an empowered state of being after cancer
It is the decision we make as we get out of bed in the morning, tired and aching
It is the ability to notice those thoughts of cancer recurrence and be at peace with them
It is the power to not let cancer define you
It is the energy in your dancing
It is the determination in your winning
It is the bravery to go outside your comfort zone
It is attitude to pick yourself up again for the tenth time when wounded again
It is the perseverance to adapt despite limitations
It is the courage to own a new body after treatment
It is sincerity that makes hugs more meaningful and just simply more
It is all about possibilities
It is noticing today and keeping balance in your life
It is getting rid of pretending and opening your heart to authenticity
It is all the rest that is left and deciding to fit it all in
It is the love that you radiate
It is your positivity of being
It is a belief in yourself beyond anyone else's
It is a faith and trust that help you calm fear
Survivorship is a state of mind that we choose every day.

The Most Beautiful Stones

The most beautiful stones
Have been worn by the wind
Washed by the waves
And polished to brilliance
By life's strongest storms

A watercolour painting using different texture techniques and paint resist applications to form the white stripes.

My Bucket List

I was looking through photos and it hit me. Do you ever look at the innocence in the photos before you were diagnosed?

Do you look into your eyes in the photo and wonder what it was like to not know what was coming? Do you look at your shape and know that it is not ever going to be like that? I looked different then – carefree. That hurts. That journey hurt.

We had just been on holiday in March break before I was diagnosed in April. I looked at the beach photos, not understanding why I couldn't see or could have felt the lump that seemed so obvious a few weeks later. I did not even like looking at those photos. I mourn the innocence and they say it is a grieving process of emotion as you lose who you were. This is difficult for others to understand. Slowly we must discover, learn to love and accept the person that you now are – not free from oncology follow up or stats but empowered to find adventure and fit all of life in. I thought I didn't have to think about this until I was old but fairness does not rule in cancer. I am one of the lucky ones I keep saying. I have purpose and a gut feeling that I am here for a reason. Not to suddenly change the world but to gently open doors that make a difference one person at a time, perhaps never quite knowing how far that reaches, but so fulfilling.

I don't like to define myself as a cancer survivor but with all that I have been through, it simply changes how I look at things so much now. Not a day goes by when those positive thinking phrases don't tap in and remind me to appreciate things and not to sweat the small stuff and there's always a way.

How long does it take to make the emotional road to recovery – to become empowered from the incredibly fearful person I was, who pushed boundaries with my own thinking phrases? Life only makes sense backwards so I will only know when I look back – am I healed yet? It is a journey and maybe always will be to some extent.

I have great goals, exciting ideas and adventures and then suddenly, like the music stops, I wish I were normal and just put my head down and work – that this didn't happen at all, I don't want these thoughts or burdens. Luckily that is brief and fleeting now – these are my cards, I own it and I look at it again and have decided that this is what makes me thrive and feel alive now with more passion for everything and it shows.

* * *

Bucket List

I've been on a journey, an exhausting long year
To the edge I have travelled, to the deepest of fear
I put back the pieces and from broken I rose
From pain and anxiety, it's courage I chose
To make myself bigger and share what I've found
That today's worth living so start looking around
Say yes to those trips that you tried to delay
Life's an adventure starting today
I love that feeling of riding deep snow
Say yes to your fears, you know where you'll go
Past boundaries set before cancer came
Overcoming your limits, life wont be the same
Swimming for medals or running a race
Winning in tennis, new battles you face
Travelling to Europe and tasting the wine
Or watching world tennis at the baseline
Surfing in Maui under blue sky
Wind on my face as I parasail high
Its a bucket list of places and things I must do
Loving life on a journey, that's the new you
Cancer's a memory hoping not to return
But the gift that it leaves is what we can learn.

Are you a Survivor or even a Thriver?

One day a person asked me how I defined the term survivor. It was a great question. It is an attitude was my answer – it is different for everybody. That took me back to the time of my war in chemo – to fight the cancer dragon with all my might.

"To carry on despite hardships or trauma, a person who copes with a bad situation and who gets through where others have failed." I survived.

I hated the word survivor when I was going through treatment. I was never going to tell myself I was free of this disease when stats and follow-ups were bombarding me. It was a word people wanted to use. I put on the yellow t-shirt for my team as we walked the relay for life after my first chemo treatment but I did not feel that I had survived cancer. I was angry that nobody could see the shadow of recurrence that we live with after cancer treatment.

Then I understood how I could wear that pink ribbon – my attitude of perseverance and determination, an attitude of fight and fury to defy this illness and give it your all. It was not to predict the future. So, at the end of all the surgeries and chemo, finally I survived. As I walked out of the war zone, numb and afraid, I had survived everything they had thrown at me.

Can someone who is living with cancer be a survivor? My Dad is a survivor everyday now. An attitude to cope with the difficulties they face in living with cancer and to rise above it where others may fail is surviving but I would have to qualify that to Thriving.

So maybe I am not just a Survivor, but also a Thriver – not just to beat away those thoughts of recurrence or another new cancer, but also to use its memory to make my day better and influence those around me.

Survivor or Thriver?

How do you define the will to survive?
Like swimming a storm to stay alive
News that hit so hard I froze
But from that hurt, its forwards I chose
Its not a forecast to forever be free
But a fighting attitude will always be me
I did survive that cancer fight
Where I kicked butt with all my might
To survive is an attitude is what I say
Making the most of every day
Finding the strength from that deep hole
Determined with toughness deep in your soul
Wear the t-shirt; show that spirit to survive
Because we choose everyday not to live but to Thrive.

Relay for life

United we stand and walk for a cause
That cancer hit us to make our lives pause
My year of recovery transformed me
To enjoy every day, a great place to be
Grateful for getting back what was taken away
My work and my tennis, to swim and now say
That I love the new me, radiant and bright
Let go of my stress and grew strong in my fight
And now teach the world to start looking around
And notice those things they wouldn't have found
Like the person at work or those in a car
They may have burdens yet a smile can go far
Its great to cheer up an ordinary face
Inspire and punch sky as we spiritually embrace
That we have fought cancer and come out on top
A spirit as warriors that no one can stop.

Growing Old Is A Beautiful Thing

As I always remind patients who complain of the aches that come with aging – growing old is a privilege that must not be assumed.

I want to grow old, see wrinkles and say
Remember the cancer that long ago day
Life's an adventure so when I reflect
My list will be full with everything checked
I'll parasail, zip line and do things I fear
You never know how your path may now steer
Pause in the day; see the beauty of now
Enrich and enjoy, don't forget how
There's always a way when spirit is strong
Inspire and give back is the way to move on
Take opportunities as they unfold
So fulfilled I will be when I get old
As people are aging they often complain
The beauty of living, I remind them again
Getting old is a privilege is now what I say
So celebrate milestones and every birthday!

Sparkle

Inspired by a conversation, one of those people who change you, a saying that belongs to me:

> She who leaves a trail of glitter
> Is never forgotten

You find these people in a few moments of conversation. Those people you feel connected to and think in the same philosophy. Choosing to look at the constructive side of things takes noticing your thoughts and putting the positive sticker over top of the doubtful one and replacing it when we are ready to move forwards.

It is energy of positivity that we chose to build. It is the thought that says yes to uncomfortable decisions – the ones where it is safer to say no but that choice will not change you. Improving means doing things outside comfort zones then realizing your strength and letting go of mistakes. There are days of quiet and inner solitude that we all need to replenish but combine that with the soul to dare. It is this inner push of attitude, that infectious positive energy that people remember more than the clothes or hair. It is our SPARKLE.

Sparkle

Sparkle is an energy caught in a star
The dare in my soul that took me so far
A spirit you see that inspires your mind
A positive energy, so contagious to find
Sparkle is happiness, thinking that way
Finding the goodness and zest in the day
Its attitude to live and help others see
The radiance of light from such energy
Don't forget what defines you- its not surface deep
The sparkle of spirit is the memory they keep
As we walk through life, put aside fear
Trust your spirit and sparkle and the path will appear.

Spirit

"I now wear my spirit, not my wig"

I was inspired to write this after seeing the adaptive skiers take on the mountain with attitude and realize the spirit they choose every day to overcome hurdles. Spirit of survivorship is around us every day.

Who are those who chose to be
A spirit in adversity
What feeds that spirit, lights that fire
A will to fight and strength inspire
On one ski they master snow
Sleds on ice, their spirits glow
I learn from them as they show me how
To take that spirit and use it now
Smile when bald and believe in you
And soon that spirit inspires more too
Be confident to love the skin you're in
With head held high, let your path begin
In helping others, that joy fulfills
A perfect remedy to fight all ills
The strength to make you come alive
With passion for life on which we thrive

Only In The Darkness Are You Able To See The Stars

As treatment ended, it was desperately hard to think I would be all right. However, just like the runner who reaches the finish line tape, I had to raise my arms and feel the accomplishment of climbing that huge mountain. I still had more to go but we must celebrate milestones, always.

It is only in the deepest, darkest places that you learn the beauty of light. That is why this was painted at night.

Only in the darkness
Are you able to see the stars

(art Therapy post Cancer)   AG

You Can't Change The World – Not Everyone Is Ready To Listen

There's a time for readiness – not everyone is there. You think you can make everyone realize that time can stand still when you least expect it – that your calendar full of appointments can dissolve in a phone call, that the only really important things are family and friends but not everyone is ready for that. Sometimes you can't change people until they are ready to listen. Maybe that's why we relate to survivors – they had that wake up call – any adversity and they know what it's like for all the balls to fall. I remember being almost jealous of the people who didn't think that could happen to them because that used to be me! Now I am changed, not by choice, cancer happened. I chose to fight; I chose to notice my second chance.

When asked what was the most significant thing I did in India, I recall one day at Mother Theresa's. We organized health checks on all the 150 residents. There was a resident who was so afraid to come to me. These people were abandoned after countless abuse, disease or tragedy. Who knows what her past held. She was so afraid, so I knelt on the floor to reassure her as she cried. With no language, a gentle voice and hand of connection I calmed her to examine her and she stopped fighting. It was a priceless moment and so moving in a bond of trust and reassurance – that's what it is all about. That's the humility we must never lose.

Then the speech for relay for life – my story doesn't feel like it defines me as much now, scarred and tested – my attitude still does. Then there was the opportunity to convey to others how to look differently at life because I had to – a poem that stings from the heart because it is just plain real.

It is not about those you can't change – I read them everywhere, comments on pre-vivor surgery – those cynical people will always be there. I want everyone to wake up to life's fragility. But, it is a choice. We can choose to focus on the many who do change as we realize precious time and priorities. Now follow your heart, change in that direction. I want to understand how our mind sorts this mountain of results into a forward nd help others to find their path. This path is good. I can feel makes sense; time will make it happen if you open the doors.

And remember a few more things each day:
The best way to show thanks is to use it no matter if its macaroni necklaces
Filter your statements before you say it
There's only a first time to notice a haircut – make it a compliment
Hang out with positive people – you rub off on each other
Simplify special times
Compliment their win, don't explain your loss
Listen, don't just talk
When you help, stick with it to the end
Keep a list of people to check up on
Everyone is a kid at heart – find that
Count the ways you love them – it conquers all
Forgive yourself for mistakes – that's how you learn
Never ever forget the gift of a second chance
Take the time to book nothing
Don't feel guilty
Make time otherwise it disappears
Change priorities
Do family breakfast
Sleeping in is a precious luxury sometimes
Trust your intuition
You are what you do, not what you say
Stay humble, always – that's authenticity
Making change may need you to step up to the plate
Never be too busy to visit
Honesty sleeps well

Everything And Nothing

Why go to India?

Before cancer, my life was perfect and safe with everything I had wanted and worked hard for. Like an accelerator pedal, when I worked harder, I got more. Cancer blindsided me and knocked me senseless with so many pieces of difficult news. I lost control and made decisions so far from my comfort zone that I lost track of who I was.

Much of going to India was exploring a new person in me. It was about not being defeated, finding control again, recalibrating fear and going so far from my comfort zone that I surprised my own limitations. I wanted to prove to myself that cancer did not destroy my inner spirit and this was a chance to rekindle that.

I was assigned to work in Mother Theresa's Home for the Dying and Destitute. I was accepted into a pioneering group of cancer survivors who held the same willpower of discovery after cancer on a journey to immerse ourselves into the community and in giving back we would learn the beauty of spirit.

It is difficult to put it into words but I think feelings do a better job: I learned so much from those who have nothing, yet are content with everything at the same time.

People may say it is so crowded or dirty or poor. But look beyond that and you see family – everyone has respect, everyone has a title, there is pride in your family and happiness in having them around you.

At Mother Teresa's the community of abandoned were one big family. We drove through the gate of The Missionaries Of Charity, through fields of potatoes, farmed by the residents at Mother Teresa's Home. As we arrived, the floors were being cleaned with buckets of water, washed down entirely, smelling of disinfectant, residents sweeping the water down the drains with bunches of palm leaves. Our arrival at 8 am was mid morning for them – their day begins with breakfast and mass then on to chores. All are dressed and the 65 beds in one room are neatly made and colourful on the thin iron cots that are 6 inches apart. The severely disabled are in wheelchairs, often adapted using old garden chairs for the seats that have long ago rotted away or broken. "Namaste" as we greeted the residents – they were so excited to see us. The sisters are tireless. Working from dawn to dusk – medications, serving meals, ensuring that the most abled fed the disabled and the routine of plate washing and cleaning repeated after every meal.

We all have limits of comfort – whether it is dealing with the lice, feeding or dealing with the most disabled or even washing the feet of the residents since they did not all wear shoes and very few actually had any that matched or fit. Whatever our limits, the Sisters Of Charity had limits beyond anything we can imagine. The work was their soul and they wanted no acknowledgment or reward more than to serve. In India, everywhere you look – people had nothing, but still had so much: hope, love, family, spirit, togetherness, happiness.

On another occasion on our busy trip, we had the privilege of meeting the leader of Cansupport – a cancer support group and society. She had been there, tasted the edge of life and suffered through cancer then came back to India to change the attitude towards cancer. The culture in India is changing to be more westernized in medical care but it is expensive and for those who survive day to day, the treatment costs are prohibitive or staying near a government hospital is isolating and unaffordable. In India, there is more cancer presenting at a later stage – estimates of 80% at stage 3 and 4. Cansupport was Harmela's dream and hard work – to create and start free palliative care teams to serve these people. They are given 24 hour support, pain medication and care.

Following the interview where clearly her compassion and motivation made this happen, we were lead to a room as a panel in front of 40 workers – doctors, nurses, psychotherapists on the palliative teams.

I realized our worlds were connected – that cancer connected us and was not that far apart. When cancer cuts us to rawness, family and support are fundamental. There is much we can learn form India when it comes to family. As much as the rooms are needed to consult the entire family, they are the daily nurses too. Palliative care comes down to comfort and support, which are not so different. I was asked questions on the panel, having been on both sides – doctor and patient:

It was in one of these questions that I realized something very important – that my work was not done, my cup still empty, so much more to learn, more to do, where was my experience going to take me?

Then a question was directed to me that summed it all up:

"Do you ever feel that on this second chance, you feel like you have been given purpose?" asked one of the palliative care doctors. The compassionate spirit of these people stung me and, with tears in my eyes, I heard myself for the first time, "Yes," I said, "I do."

What a lot we have to learn. What a lot I learned from those with nothing but also with everything.

Giving back

Life is a balance; we must all leave our mark
By helping our neighbour or adventure embark
I help those through struggles, fulfilled everyday
Never imagine how it could all go away
So hard to erase the pain from the past
So I notice the small things; go slower not fast
Hang out with people with visions like you
To live to the fullest, authentically true
In Delhi I thought that in giving I'd grow
But joy of having nothing is what they would show
How wrong could I be, it turned inside out
I think we'd be better if we all tried this out
Not to go far but just look every time
At a kindness you can do in a long line
It's not just the giving that changes you
It's about seeing life from a whole new view
I look at the sea, the rocks and the sky
We are visiting earth as time marches by
See if you feel it, it's why we are here
Let your heart make a difference that makes life clear.

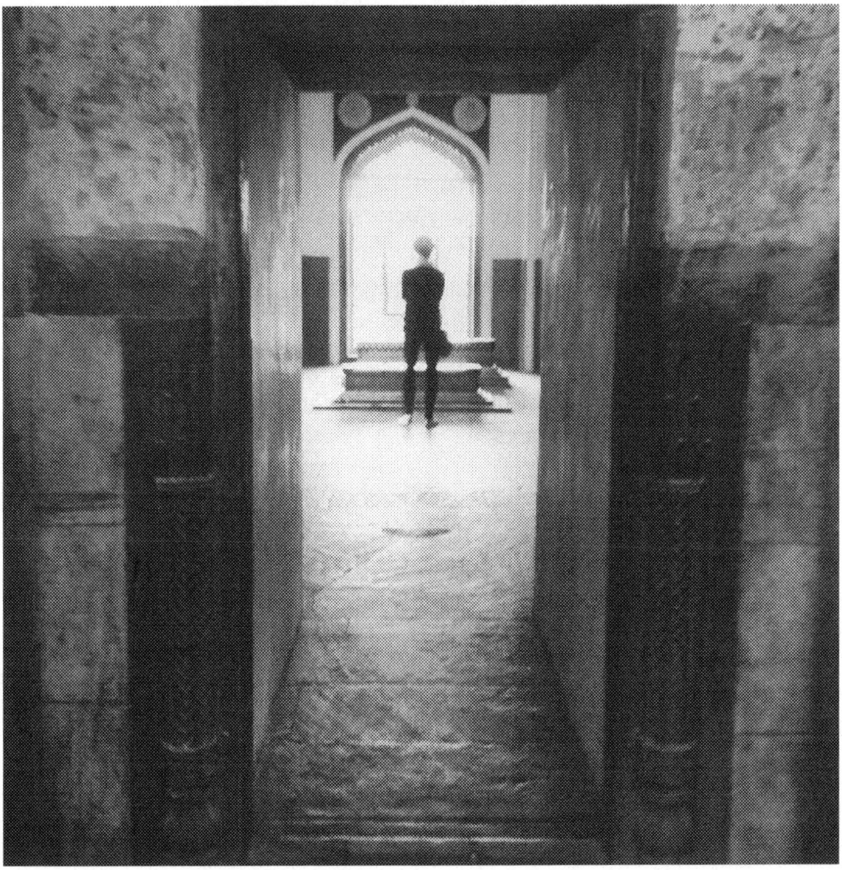

The "Used to" Person

I meet them all the time. When asked if they exercise, "I used to swim, run, dance." I am now a present day person, not to look at limitations but the possibilities and opportunities within our capabilities. What I do today is what counts yet I am different than I used to be, especially physically. It is about discovering activities that your body now prefers – try new things, get good at it and open up a different world of activities. It is about what I can do, not I used to.

    I don't want to hear about all the medals of the past as much as the great walk that you took yesterday with the dog or the new zumba class you discovered to shake the energy away because the knees don't like running. I want to discover art and not focus on the painful feet. Each day is a fresh discovery, a gift of a second chance and not about what we used to and now can't do. So join me in being "today" people, leaving the "used to" attitude in the past and using your talent to be I am:

* * *

"Used To" Poem

Did you ever meet "I used to"
Who didn't live the now
Did he notice all my broken parts
Having fun and wonder how
To define yourself by the past
You will not make goals today
Achieving gives us confidence
You must discover your new way
Don't tell me of your trophies
Or how much you used to dance
Try paddleboard, a photo course
Pilates – now's your chance
So if you hurt or think you're done
Just ask me what to do
Find your talent, set new goals
Be "I am", not "I used to."

Define Yourself

Do you think cancer defines you – think again? I love definitions and keep a loyal list of my favourites to keep with me and give me energy when it dips or I am hurting a bit too much.

Tenacity – to hold on, stay on the course – to want it, know that you will make it, even when it is rough.

Remember those days: We still have it. We still need it …

There I was in the water, helping my little 10 year old nephew get up on water-skis – he tried and tried then I remembered the secret – "just one more second" I told him. We repeated it together as I helped the skis back on. When you feel like letting go, trust me, hold on for one more second. I remember that feeling. Yes, out of the water he flew, scared and thrilled all mixed together. It is this tenacity that we have – hold on that rope just a bit longer.

Motivation – stimulus or influence, incentive or drive.

Give yourself something to aim for – sign up for that run, join a golf group, learn a language and travel there, take an art course, learn an instrument, make it possible, not big but definitely fun – this is your chance.

Strength – Firmness or courage, mentally powerful, decisively unyielding, firm or uncompromising, wilful – capacity for exertion or endurance, power to resist force, solidity, toughness.

I am not talking about lifting weights here – I have trouble with opening a wine bottle some days but look out – willpower is what I am talking about – the strength in the fight is in your soul, not just your muscles.

Possible – Being within the limits of ability, capacity or realization but a difficult task.

Could you knock me down enough from my tennis court – I just need possible and something in between to get there. It is about setting small goals to get you there – finding a friend to hit with, walk with, adapting your workplace, taking it in small strides and you will get there – Just need Possible.

Support – To bear or hold up, sustain or withstand under trial or affliction, to give aid.

They say support is one of the biggest predictors of success beyond the medical treatment of cancer. What would we do without support? As we receive, so we in turn will give back – the immensity of support is felt so deeply that when our storm has settled, it feels good to pass it on to others in need. In giving we are fulfilled.

Journey – An experience that leaves you changed; a trail of experience – from here to there.

I remember hating the word "journey" when I was in treatment – I said journey sounded like a nice walk in the park – this was a %#&* roller coaster of sickness, nausea and pain – I certainly could not see a nice journey! Now I realize how different I am – one of those definitions, I can only see as I look back from a distance. Yes I am changed from that awful year – journey – yes it is.

Endurance – The ability to withstand hardship or adversity, especially the ability to sustain a prolonged stressful effort or activity.

You may think of Olympic athletes when you read this definition – no, it is bigger than that. It is to get through the fear, pain, sickness, to watch family suffer when you are helpless, to push on when some doubt, to find the endurance to last the course and come back – yes you did run a marathon –congratulations on your endurance to climb mountains.

Perseverance – steady persistence in a course of action, a purpose, and a state, especially in spite of difficulties, obstacles, or discouragement.

What great quality perseverance is? It is about getting up for the tenth time after you have fallen again and again – so weakened but hardened to reach the end, even when weak; not to quit. It is a steadfast forwards motion – perseverance does not hesitate or look back despite adversity. It is up hill, through the wind and rain, battered and cold. Getting there – that is perseverance.

Determination – The psychological definition of determination is the condition of being determined; resoluteness, a resolute movement towards some object or end. It has emotional qualities of ambition to reach a difficult target with wilfulness balanced by the discipline of hard work to achieve it. It is a quality of success or survival. It is an inner belief despite difficulties that you will reach your desired outcome – we post pictures of determination to remind us of the inner strength and fortitude in determination. Who said it was easy?

What lies in front of us and what lies behind us are small compared to what lies within us.

Resilience – ability to recover from illness, adversity or the like – the power to return to the correct form after being bent. Post-traumatic growth.

This is where I live now – post-traumatic growth. I am not the same – not moulded back into shape after being bent; no, I am stronger – finding mindfulness, positive thinking tools and cognitive behavioural methods to notice thoughts and stick better ones in their place when going in the wrong direction. I hope I don't have to put resilience to the test again but cancer is a shadow – we all know that so I practice my tools every day and find good places to go to find peace in my mind.

Off I go now as I work on an on-line art therapy course that is creatively taking me to that great place of mindful freedom – a great place to keep life in balance. I am working on collaging and painting my quotes and definitions with acrylic medium on canvas.

DON'T LET CANCER DEFINE YOU – DEFINE YOURSELF.

Cut And Keep

My Positive Thinking cards are to be kept in a purse, a chemo bag or in a car to pull out and remind you to change your thinking. Cut these and put them in a place where you can grab them and remind yourself to think differently.

Positive Thinking Card 1
Things to Remember

Laugh at myself. Laugh at mistakes. Get up, put make up on, show up for life. Exercise. Enjoy every moment, live for today. Laugh again. Don't sweat the small stuff. If it didn't hurt anyone, leave it in the past. Worry only about the things that you can change. Don't complain, take a pill. Ask for help. Order it online when you feel lousy. Play tennis. Talk to those people who make you feel good. Laugh at those cravings. Remember your eyebrow pencil in your purse. There's always a way. Play the cards you are dealt. Perseverance. Love your job, if you don't, change it. Control stress. When it upsets you, write it down, it works. Heal thyself mentally too, chemo fog is real. Make lists, make to do lists. Smile, you look better. Put away the black clothes. Say yes more than you want to, you'll be surprised at the results. Swim. Remember the best people in the world and how much they are there for you, always and always.

**Positive Thinking Card 2
More Things To Remember**

One day at a time. Everyone has a story. Allow more time. Inspire. Destiny. Every day is a special day – never take it for granted. Read. Push yourself – it feels great. You have great gifts – share them. Don't forget your family – they are amazing. Be a "yes man". Share the joy of life. Write. Step beyond your comfort zone – you'll be proud of yourself. Love the skin you are in – don't be jealous. Rest and take in the moment. Life is what you make it. Don't say words that you will regret. Say sorry. Say thank you. Create. Don't compare. Take the time to visit. Priorities. Be grateful. Deal with something that bothers you. Don't blame others. Don't expect others to understand how you feel. Some people say the wrong thing – don't be angry. Positive attitude. Friends are always there. Change things that are negative. Strength and courage prevail. Perseverance. Time heals. Believe in yourself. Love myself as I am. Remember your spiritual side.

Positive Thinking Card 3
Things to Remember Moving On

Sleep on it – its better in the morning. Remember your new path. You got through last year – you can get through anything. Inspire. Book coffee with a friend. Visit. Take a moment to call – it is worth a thousand thoughts. Healing takes 6 weeks. Go beyond your comfort zone- you'll be proud of yourself. Take more time. Give yourself permission to play. Book art time. Book reading time. Play tennis. Go to that place in your head where time stands still. Balance. Make things happen – they don't always fall in your lap. Make to do lists. Write. Forgive yourself. You are not perfect- don't expect perfect. Only the healthy me is helpful. Lead with your heart. You are rare. Be patient of your healing. Do what you can do. Speak out to relieve the burden. Don't look back unless to gain wisdom. Fear is part of me but lives quietly in peace. Choose to be happy. All you can do is always enough. Focus on positives. Trust yourself. Keep writing.

Positive Thinking Card 4
No Excuses

No Excuses. There's always a way. Choose to be happy. Pay forward kindness. Balance. Believe in yourself. Speak with your actions – be a role model. Save thank you cards – know that you are loved. Celebrate everyday. Don't complain – step up to the plate. Focus on the comeback one step at a time – that's life. Don't be afraid of embarrassment – you'll miss the chance of success. When life throws you curve balls – learn to hit them back. No need for medals – fulfillment comes from within. Miracles are not always what you wish for – they may be right in front of you. Give compliments. Give a card – because. Paint sunflowers. Wear your heart on your sleeve – believe in yourself. Think of everything you love. If you focus on the negative, you miss the thousand positive things that can happen. Take educated risks. Looking after everyone, includes yourself. Fear is the opposite of trust. Make a difference. Be the one. Make someone's day. Exercise cleanses the chaos. Exercise the mind- keep learning. Believe strengths are bigger than weaknesses. Stay grounded. Wear your spirit, not your wig.

Positive Thinking Card 5
Words of Wisdom

Trust your intuition. Where there's a will, there's a way. Laugh. Give yourself permission to rest. Look at what you can do. Face the bumps with a smile. Life is full of surprises – be adaptable. Keep learning. Make achievable goals. Stay connected. Ask for help. Make lists. Choose to be happy. Work out to great music. Don't procrastinate. Make it happen. The best things in life are free. Don't be afraid to begin. Book friends time. Style points count – make the effort. Pick up the phone and call. Be young at heart. No regrets. Take different routes. Try new things. Challenge yourself. Book walk and talk time together. Positive energy is contagious. Be authentic. Commit. Hang out with positive people. Rise above adversity. Give back. Love the new you – bigger by experience. Feel good moments – freeze frame. It's all about the come back, show them it's possible. Believe in yourself when it's hard. Determination wins. Switch on your second engine when it seems hard.

Positive Thinking Card 6
Resilience

Resilience is post-traumatic growth. Life only makes sense backwards. I will manage – just control what you can. Adapt. Do your best, people understand you are human. Coffee. Take a walk. Rules weren't made to be personal. Look at the big picture. I am an emotional survivor. Break it down into pieces that are reachable. Make a list – check it off. Print a calendar. Be prepared. Laugh. Bake and have fun with the adventure. Look around – I am blessed. Shop on line. Chat online. Lower expectations. Enjoy the day in minutes. Get an app for that. Watch expiry dates. Download a movie for hospital waits. Hang out with positive people. Don't cancel getting together with friends. Keep the tennis game. Email works. It will work out in the end – trust that. These are just bumps in the road. Own it. Work with it. Live. Plan a trip. Stay positive. Create. Paint. Share the excitement. Life is great – feel it. Self check too. Think of solutions not problems. Mothers say wise things. Keep thoughts constructive, not destructive. Say thank you every day.

Positive Thinking Card 7
Remember What I Have Got

LOVE – someone who shows his love, not just says it – my rock. **SUPPORT** – they understand and protect me- my colleagues, my friends. **DETERMINATION** – showing I can do it, no excuses. **FITNESS** – look how far I have come – looking good, feeling great, overcome obstacles. **POSITIVE ATTITUDE** – there's always a way, adapt. **INTELLIGENCE** – learn new things, get it back, think fast, try hard. **FRIENDS** – they all appeared when I needed them most. **MY JOB** – my vocation, to make a difference, how it felt to loose that then get it back. **SINCERITY** – authenticity is the only way to be. **EMPATHY** – it stings because you've been there but your path is your own. **STRENGTH** – of mind and body never tested so much. **CREATIVITY** – the silent therapy within my brain. **EXPERIENCE** – to be on both sides and pass on the coping tools, to understand. **PERMISSION** – to rest, to play, to be enough. **FAMILY** – always there, always a shoulder to lean on. **SPIRIT** – contagious, adventurous, fit it all in, smile. **PURPOSE** – believe in yourself and your path.

Positive Thinking Card 8
Own it

Go beyond your comfort zone, you'll be proud of yourself. Be amazed. Be inspired. Be humbled. Don't let time run out, fit it all in. Prove that you can do it. Take educated risks. No regrets or maybe's. Be prepared but do it. Be proud of myself. Learn new things. You can do it, make it happen. Think of a way. Flip your thinking. Determination is a forwards direction. Challenge yourself. Be the change. Own it – share it- inspire with it. Goalify. Notice your thinking. Priorities. Push yourself. Finish. Examine guilty feelings and correct them. Be kind to yourself too. Remember to laugh. Doors open – see them – walk through them. Learn new things. Be the change. Own your disease. Share the wisdom. Inspire with your change.

Thinking Card 9
Forgive Yourself

Forgive yourself – you are not the first one to make that mistake. Put things in perspective. Change things. Plan ahead – just not too far. Have a plan B. Write down the day. Put it in the calendar immediately. Copy to everyone. Time has more minutes than you think. Remember the good stuff. Be sincere. Learn new things when old ones don't work. Rest your mind. Deal with the inbox – into the outbox. Be the change you talk about. Give people a chance to try. Prepare the night before. Grow vegetables. Learn about tea. Sew and create. Scrabble. Old movies together. Paddleboard. Blaze new trails. Influence others. It is what it is – some things can't change. Attitude is controllable. Tomorrow is a brand new day. A journey together feels so much better. Make a new wish every day. You can find light in the darkest places. Run, sweat, peace. Count good things. Run, sweat, feel better. Being alone sometimes feels good, sometimes not good – be OK with that. Permission to have a nap. Talking books. Love that person who holds your hand at every finish line! Sometimes, saying yes makes extraordinary memories – that's worth it. Figure it out. Delegate. Remarkable people do not just happen.

Positive Thinking Card 10
Remember The Process

Remember the process, not just the result. Put a value on that. Daily gratitude. Daily intentions. Meditation in movement. Don't forecast. Look at stumbling blocks differently. Forgive even the hardest things. If it's not good for you, let go of that thought. You are genuine – the right people see you for that. Don't prejudge. Go with the flow. Self check thinking. Filter words. Making change is not instant. Be in the present. Remember to celebrate everything. Try. How can you learn if you don't fail at something? Wisdom comes from learning from things that went wrong. Listen to wise people and learn from their mistakes. Trust your instincts. Believe in purpose. Believe your inner strength. Believe that worlds collide when they are supposed to and stars align. Believe that you can make a difference – that you matter. A soul to dare.

Notes and Quotes

I love to write definitions, quotes and inspiring notes. This is your handbook of encouragement, a reference in those tough times to pull forwards. Keep it near you, bookmark a poem. Write some of your favourite quotes here and make it your own.

The bird in the tree is not afraid of the branch breaking
When he trusts the strength of his own wings.

I want to inspire people
I want someone to read this and say
Because of you I didn't give up!

Notes and Quotes

Notes and Quotes

Notes and Quotes

Notes and Quotes

Notes and Quotes

Acknowledgements

Thank you to the following for my healing:

Facingcancer.ca Blog and Cancer Support Network

Look Good Feel Better Workshops

Wellspring – Cancer Support Centre
Art and Writing Therapy programs

Oakville Trafalgar Memorial Hospital Surgical Teams

Trillium Health Partners Genetics at Credit Valley Hospital and The Carlo Fidani Peel Regional Cancer Centre and my Oncology Team

My sister for her artistic cover design

My patients for unwavering support and belief in my return

My office and hospital colleagues – permission to heal

My family for their support and friends who edited and encouraged this to happen

Margaret – My Rock, always looking out for me

Appendix of Medical Terms

Adhesions – Scarring

Axillary – Armpit

Bilateral – Both sides

BRCA – **BR**east **CA**ncer gene. Mutation of this gene in BRCA1 or BRCA2 type is responsible for a very high risk of breast and ovarian cancer in approximately 5 % of breast cancer cases.

Breast MRI – Magnetic Resonance Imaging – a diagnostic imaging tool for highly suspicious cases of breast cancer.

Dissection – selective removal surgery.

In-Situ – limited cancer tumour. It is localized and cannot metastasize in its current form but has the potential to change to an invasive type of cancer.

Invasive – a cancer that is able to spread by blood or lymph tissues. There are different types and levels of aggression of these tumours.

Lymphedema – Swelling of a limb eg. arm from lymph fluid due to surgical removal or radiation of lymph nodes.

Mastectomy – Surgical breast removal. Bilateral mastectomies – both breasts surgically removed.

Metastases – cancer spread away from original primary site.

Multifocal – Many areas of primary cancer tumours.

Sentinel Node – Specific draining lymph node for the cancer tumour, evaluated by radioactive tracer and dye during surgery.

Seroma – fluid collection of lymph fluid